MAKING PEACE WITH PORN

What people are saying…

"*Making Peace with Porn* is a very important book.

"In a manner that is equal parts frank, accessible, and thorough, Vivas explains why it is that most men watch porn…and why it is that (generally) watching porn is not a bad thing.

"Vivas—a successful businesswoman, adult-industry leader, wife, mother, and self-identified feminist—debunks myths about 'porn stars' and the adult industry's inner workings. She also draws on academic studies, personal stories, and her own company's extensive sales data and online traffic to show a more nuanced picture of porn consumption. Taken together, these insights and information help readers move beyond reacting to porn and, instead, work toward engaging more in-depth considerations of adult entertainment.

"Vivas tackles a number of uncomfortable issues, including self-confidence and sexual shame. Her anecdotes and personal insights shoot straight, speaking from a place of informed individual experience.

"This book is essential reading for anyone struggling with their guy's 'relationship' with porn or just looking to become more informed about the mysterious but ultimately ordinary adult entertainment industry."

— Chauntelle Anne Tibbals, PhD, Sociologist

"Allison is the ideal author for a book like *Making Peace with Porn*. Not only does she have a long and accomplished history in the adult entertainment industry, she's also perceptive, open minded, rational, and data driven, which enables her to write objectively about a subject that is very close to her heart. She brings both an adult-industry executive and mother's perspective to her analysis, a combination that is as rare as it is valuable."

— Michael H. Klein President, *HUSTLER* LFP, Inc./Flynt Management Group, LLC

DEDICATION

✷ *To the Universe* ✷

Thank you for your yin and yang balance,
which serves to keep the world in harmony
while simultaneously causing conflict.
It is this delicate equilibrium that causes many of us women
to seek the man of our dreams while remaining
confused as to why he doesn't think the same way we do.

Without it, there would be no need for this book.

Ordering
Trade bookstores in the U.S. and Canada please contact
Publishers Group West
1700 Fourth Street, Berkeley CA 94710
Phone: (800) 788-3123   Fax: (800) 351-5073

For bulk orders please contact
Special Sales
Hunter House Inc., PO Box 2914, Alameda CA 94501-0914
Phone: (510) 899-5041   Fax: (510) 865-4295
E-mail: sales@hunterhouse.com

Individuals can order our books by calling **(800) 266-5592**
or from our website at **www.hunterhouse.com**

MAKING PEACE
with
Porn

ADULT ENTERTAINMENT
and YOUR GUY

ALLISON VIVAS

PRESIDENT OF PINK VISUAL

Copyright © 2013 by Tekco Management Group, LLC

All rights reserved. No part of this publication may be reproduced or transmitted in any form or by any means, electronic or mechanical, including photocopying and recording, or introduced into any information storage and retrieval system without the written permission of the copyright owner and the publisher of this book. Brief quotations may be used in reviews prepared for inclusion in a magazine, newspaper, or for broadcast. For further information please contact:

Hunter House Inc., Publishers
PO Box 2914
Alameda CA 94501-0914

Library of Congress Cataloging-in-Publication Data
Vivas, Allison.
Making peace with porn / Allison Vivas.
pages cm
Includes bibliographical references and index.
ISBN 978-0-89793-657-6 (trade paper) — ISBN 978-0-89793-658-3 (ebook)
1. Pornography. 2. Sexual excitement. 3. Man-woman relationships. 4. Sex. I. Title.
HQ471.V58 2013
363.4'7—dc23   2012048650

Project Credits

Cover Design: Brian Dittmar Design, Inc.	Publicity Coordinator: Martha Scarpati
Book Production: John McKercher	Special Sales Manager: Judy Hardin
Contract Editor: Amanda E. Clark	Rights Coordinator: Candace Groskreutz
Copy Editor: Kelley Blewster	Publisher's Assistant: Bronwyn Emery
Indexers: Robert and Cynthia Swanson	Customer Service Manager: Christina Sverdrup
Managing Editor: Alexandra Mummery	Order Fulfillment: Washul Lakdhon
Editorial Intern: Jordan Collins	Administrator: Theresa Nelson
Acquisitions Intern: Sally Castillo	Computer Support: Peter Eichelberger
Publisher: Kiran S. Rana	

Printed and bound by Bang Printing, Brainerd, Minnesota
Manufactured in the United States of America

9 8 7 6 5 4 3 2 1   First Edition   13 14 15 16 17

CONTENTS

★ ★ ★

AUTHOR'S NOTE

As little girls we grow up with fantasies of what our perfect life will look like, which also happens to include our perfect man (for heterosexual girls anyway). Once we find that perfect man the illusion of fantasy may wear off and we are left with reality. And that reality may include the fact that our guy watches porn whether we like it or not. Guiding yourself through the Internet for help on this subject, whether you are seeking a way to understand and accept it, or simply to cope, can be a murky, time-consuming, and frustrating experience. The Internet is filled with anonymous forum posts, men's articles, and antiporn propaganda that use hyperbole to incite fear and uncertainty. None of these resources provide the full picture, nor do they offer insight into what porn really is or why a man may enjoy it. Certainly none of them leave a woman feeling better and more sexually confident, or more knowledgeable about her position on the topic, a good approach for talking about it with her partner, or its place in her relationship.

It is my intention with this book to change that. The book offers a lot of insight regarding the adult industry, gathered from insider information and website traffic statistics used by industry pros. Ultimately, my hope is that it leads you to reevaluate any preconceived notions and expectations you may hold of yourself and your partner.

Important Note

The material in this book is intended to provide a review of information regarding pornography and adult relationships. Every effort has been made to provide accurate and dependable information. We believe that the sensuality advice given in this book poses no risk to any healthy person. However, if you have any sexually transmitted diseases, we recommend consulting your doctor before using this book.

Therefore, the publisher, authors, and editors, as well as the professionals quoted in the book, cannot be held responsible for any error, omission, professional disagreement, or dated material, and are not liable for any damage, injury, or other adverse outcome of applying any of the information resources in this book. If you have questions concerning the application of the information described in this book, consult a qualified professional.

Introduction: Porn and Us

We're all girls here, right? So let's be honest with each other. There is no one out there who ever plans for a career in the adult entertainment industry. No one, when she is a little girl, says, "When I grow up I'm going to work in porn." It just doesn't happen. It certainly wasn't that way for me.

I might be young (well, thirty-two, but don't spread that around) and blonde, and I might work in pornography, but I don't do my job in front of the cameras. If you do a Google search of my name you won't find any videos out there (don't think you would be the first one to try). Not that there is anything wrong with the women who do operate in front of the cameras (we will get to that later), but I fill a different role.

As the president of the adult entertainment studio Pink Visual, I followed a path to my career that is common across the adult industry—namely, I fell into it by chance. Even so it's a decision I am proud of and a career I enjoy. I am also aware that the industry I work in is one that inspires strong opinions, among men and women alike. Some people love pornography and think of it as a form of free expression and sexual empowerment; others absolutely hate what the industry produces. I think that's fair; it's a free country and everyone has a right to their opinions. But some of those opinions are the reason why I decided to write this book. I know there are a lot of women out there who don't understand pornography as a form of entertainment and are irritated, and possibly intimidated, by the idea (or fact) that their guy looks at the material. Or it's possible they are in complete denial about the reality that their man has watched a couple of (probably more) "dirty" movies in his life.

Let's address the elephant in the room: The man you are married to, dating, or otherwise romantically involved with looks at porn.

Now before you get mad at me over that assumption, let me point out there is a reason why you picked up this book. And more likely than not it has to do with the fact that you know my statement is true, or you secretly believe that maybe there is a hint of truth in it and you need a little convincing.

Regardless of what camp you are in, please know that I have been in your shoes. Frankly, I thought my "Mr. Right" was the one guy in the world who didn't look at porn. I operated under that notion until… well…he asked me to watch it with him. And get this: I cried.

So much for that illusion, right?

Now you are probably saying, "Wait a second Allison, you *work* in the adult entertainment industry! How could you *cry* over the fact that your guy looks at porn videos?"

Let me answer that. I haven't always been the president of an adult studio. And there was a time when I didn't know anything about pornography, its role in men's lives, and its impact on our society. These are all things I have learned over time and in the course of my employment with Pink Visual.

I'm a Normal Girl, I Just Happen to Work in Porn

If you were to get to know me, which you will throughout this book, you would find that my background is pretty normal. I come from a middle-class family. I grew up with two parents in a drama-free household. I was an honors student in high school and graduated cum laude from the University of Arizona. I might describe myself as a tomboy of sorts; I participated in sports and had a particular knack for softball and soccer. I suppose you could say that I was relatively popular throughout school. I was outgoing, had plenty of friends, and didn't really date much. I was part of the Internet age. I remember having a dial-up AOL account, through which I communicated regularly with my friends via AOL Instant Messenger. Even though I was part of the first generation of kids who had the bulky old desktop computers in their bedrooms or dorm rooms, it would never have occurred to me to look for Internet porn on it. Porn wasn't on my radar, and I wasn't aware that it was on anyone else's radar either.

All in all, if you took one look at my upbringing, or even who I am today, you would say I was pretty typical. I don't have any "baggage" or "daddy issues" that critics of the industry like to rail about, nor am I a "damaged" woman. Without getting into some heavy psychoanalysis it's safe to say that some of those blanket statements are little more than that: assumptions and myths about what the people who work in the industry look like or who they are as individuals. We'll talk more about that later.

The point I'm trying to make is that while growing up and becoming an adult I was a normal girl. When I graduated from college I was still pretty innocent by most standards. I was more interested in finding "The One" than in bouncing from guy to guy as a serial dater, and, ultimately, I did that. I found my Mr. Right, who was perfect for me in every way.

Let me state for the record that this was the *same* Mr. Right who asked me to watch porn with him.

"You Want Me to Do *What*?"

When he made this request, and right before I broke into tears, tons of thoughts rushed through my head. I thought, "How can he like this stuff? Does he want me to look like that? Does he want me to be with someone else when we are…you know? Does he want me to do all of those things in bed? Does he think I need a boob job?" The list goes on. Before that moment I had honestly thought I'd found the one guy on the face of the planet who had no interest in the stuff. I was so upset. And I got over it.

I even married him. I'm still with him today. And we have two perfectly normal and wonderful kids.

Of course, there is a path between my crying over being propositioned with pornography and the life I lead today. And it's been an education. I hope to be able to give you some insight into that education, both to help you understand what pornography actually means to your man and also to help improve your relationship.

It's like this: We women can very easily choose to shame our guy over his tendency to look at pornography, a type of entertainment that is, in fact, very natural to men's biology and their sexual makeup, or we can choose to be mature about it. We can probably also even learn from the simple acknowledgement that it's okay for a guy to be turned on by this type of material.

Personally, I believe that learning the truth about the dynamic between men and porn can provide any woman with a lot of great knowledge and awareness, not only about the man in her life but also about herself as a woman. How do I know? Because I used to think like a lot of other women do, and I once had only negative opinions about why men like porn, notions that I have since learned are utterly false. The way I got schooled on this topic, of course, was by working in the adult entertainment industry and examining the business and psychology behind it. Trust me when I say it's not as scary as some critics out there would have you believe. Through my ten-plus years of experience at Pink Visual I have had the opportunity to evaluate data, and I have been privy to some very interesting conversations with men and women both inside and outside of the industry. I think I have figured out the riddle many women face related to men and porn, and it is this I want to share with you.

Knowledge Is Power and Leads to Understanding

As an industry insider I have access to a great deal of valuable data about the porn-viewing habits of men. At Pink Visual and around the industry we can identify and track porn-consumption trends that most guys won't openly discuss, in part because they know that the women in their lives won't "get it," and they fear being judged and shamed for their behavior and their fantasies by those whom they love.

Think about it, ladies: Just as the idea of what happens in a porno film might make you feel nervous, self-conscious, or perhaps ashamed of your sexuality, the same holds true for your husband, boyfriend, or partner. He may feel just as guilty, embarrassed, or nervous about pornography as you do, but a lot of that is because he doesn't know how to talk to you about it or about why certain things in pornography turn him on. In turn, you feel defensive or upset and don't understand his natural inclination to view the material.

And that is where the real shame lies. There are so many people who are so closed-minded to the idea that there's anything positive that can come from watching porn—or from considering what we can learn from men's porn-viewing habits—that these discussions never even occur. The topic never has the opportunity to be broached. Frankly, this sort of data has tremendous potential to help women better understand men, themselves, and their views toward sex, and to accept their romantic relationships on a more positive level. I have always been a big believer in the idea that knowledge—all knowledge—is empowering. Gaining an understanding of adult entertainment and its place in our lives and culture can make it easier for conversations about sex and relationships to take place.

There's no denying that pornography is a polarizing subject, but I think you will find that once you open your mind and start to consider the reality behind this form of entertainment, instead of simply subscribing to preconceived notions or negative mythologies that critics like to focus on and preach about, you will discover that there is more to be achieved by discussing pornography than there is by denying its existence or shunning it completely.

This book relates the story of my own growth around pornography, both personally and professionally, and how that journey has led me to be a more confident and stronger woman. I reveal truths about the industry, both positive and negative. And I attempt to make all of this easy to relate to by comparing porn to shoe shopping and including third-party research about sexuality. I also refer to correspondence we have received at Pink Visual. I know that readers of this book rarely, if ever, will have been exposed to this sort of "insider" information, and I think you will find it valuable. Not only will it provide insight, but it might just make you laugh. I hope you will go on your own journey as you read this book, coming out more confident and with a better understanding of your guy.

1 | "My Guy Watches Porn—What's Wrong with Him?"

So your guy watches porn. Or maybe you're suffering through denial that he does. You've probably had a few sleepless nights or have exchanged some bitter words about his porn-viewing habits, but it's not working. He isn't getting it, and you are more than bothered by the fact that he is clearly clueless that his behavior is disgusting and foul. Let's just say you are pretty pissed off.

He continues to look at porn videos despite the fact that he knows it upsets you, and he's probably brushed you off multiple times with a rude dismissal, saying that you are overreacting about nothing—that porn is just porn, it's no big deal.

Safe to say you think his brush-off is less than sufficient, and you are also, at this point, toying with the idea that something is not right with him—something is wrong with his head, he's a pervert, sexually deviant, or worse.

Whoa! Hold on just a minute there. Cool it, sister, and rein in your very active imagination. We need to inject a bit of logic at this point, and you need to take a couple of deep breaths, put your head between your knees, think some calming thoughts, and *relax*!

Okay, so you are upset about your guy's casual attitude toward pornography and the fact that he doesn't seem very sensitive to the idea that it makes you upset and uncomfortable. To start (and I'm not trying to take his side just because I run an adult studio and he buys the products my industry produces; I have solidarity with you, babe, trust me), your guy isn't very good at explaining his porn-viewing habits because he is self-conscious about them and is especially worried that you know what he does on his computer. He might be thinking some crazy thoughts about your fights over pornography and the way you feel about the entertainment he subscribes to. He might be thinking that you'll never understand him completely or understand why, as a guy, he watches porn. Maybe the mere idea of letting you control that part of his life is bothersome, frustrating, and confusing. He thinks pornography is harmless. It very well might be, but his lack of communication with you about it is causing harm. Moreover, he might even realize he is doing a bad job of expressing himself, which makes him not only upset but also something akin to ashamed. It's important for you to realize that some of this shame is about masturbation and was probably present before you came into the picture. Maybe as a teenager or young man living at home he had to awkwardly hide his activities from his mom, so it's no wonder he has a hard time talking about his pornography viewing to another important woman in his life.

Since most guys aren't voluntarily letting women in on why exactly they watch porn and what they really think about it, I'll help provide some insight on their behalf. I am doing this so you can relax and feel reassured that your guy is like every other guy in America. He is perfectly normal for watching porn. You don't have to worry any longer that he is a pervert, a deviant, or wants you to be with another woman or get a boob job. He is just a normal guy.

I'm Not Just Saying This Because I Work for a Porn Company—It's True!

This isn't just made-up reasoning. It's an analysis of the information that is now available to the public based on Internet browsing data and statistics. While it's true that the Internet has opened up the audience for the product created by my company, Pink Visual, and other adult entertainment companies, the Internet also affords us the opportunity to better understand people's habits around pornography. In the pre-Internet days there was no way to know what percentage of sexually active men were purchasing or renting adult videos or stashing porno magazines in secret places. But now we have the ability not only to know these numbers but also to analyze the data. All that information is much more easily accessible.

I tell you this because having access to the data benefits you and your understanding of pornography and its role in your romantic relationship. This is good news, ladies!

For example, did you know there are almost double the number of Google searches for the term "porn" than there are for the search terms "music" and "sports" combined? Looking at Figure 1.1 on the next page you can see that even on the days when Apple releases its newest iPhone (or iPad or whatever), the term "iPhone" (or "iPad," etc.) spikes up to just surpass the number of daily searches for "porn."[1]

Google has a cool tool called Google Trends that is available to the public. Give it a whirl yourself. Go to www.google.com/trends, enter the search term "XXX," and compare it to the search query "Super Bowl," for instance. By doing this you can see how popular the search

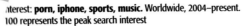

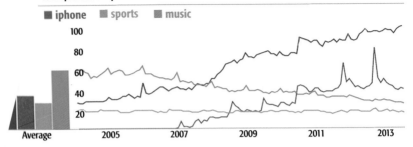

FIGURE 1.1 A chart from Google Trends depicting web search trends of "porn," "iphone," "sports," and "music."

term "Super Bowl" is on Super Bowl Sunday. Just think about it. On Super Bowl Sunday the majority of men, as well as many women, are taking an interest in the event and have their Web-capable mobile phones nearby, enabling them to look up anything Super Bowl-related, including commercials. That's a lot of people looking up "Super Bowl." However, to put everything in perspective, what stands out is the fact that the term "XXX" has that search volume *every single day of the year*. And "XXX" does only one-third of the search volume that the term "porn" does. For those of you who didn't immediately put this book down to check out the website, Figure 1.2 is a better image of what I'm talking about,[2] but do try it. Plug in some search terms relating to your interests and see how they compare to "porn."

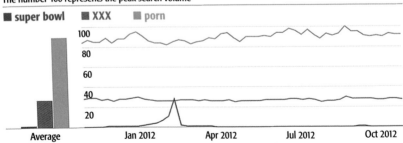

FIGURE 1.2 Google Trends results comparing the search quantities for "Super Bowl," "porn," and "xxx."

If you are a stats junkie, you might also enjoy another book about a similar topic titled *A Billion Wicked Thoughts*. Written by neuroscientists Ogi Ogas and Sai Gaddam, it provides insights from web-search trends into the minds of both men and women. And there are many more statistics and studies out there and available to the public. Plenty of clinical studies on online pornography have been conducted and are accessible by any interested person. However, if you don't feel like looking up the latest research, consider the general consensus that pornography viewing accounts for approximately 30 percent of all traffic on the Internet.[3] That's right! I said *all* traffic!

Scientifically Speaking, It's Not an Anomaly

Meanwhile, in another recent study, researchers at the University of Montreal attempted to compare the views of men who watched porn to the views of men who hadn't watched porn. I say they *attempted* to carry out the study because they weren't able to actually find any members of the latter category.

I'll say that again. Scientific researchers couldn't find a single man who would admit to not watching porn. Granted, the study focused on men in their twenties, but it included both single men and men who stated they were currently involved in a romantic relationship.[4]

To sum it all up, current conservative estimates show that, worldwide, a hundred million people per day look at pornography, and roughly 95 percent of that number is male. That's ninety-five million men who look at porn on the Internet every day. This number doesn't include pay-per-view numbers, viewing booths at adult sex shops, adult movie theaters (yes, a few of those dinosaurs are still around), watching porn on DVD or video in the privacy of one's home, or even looking at "dirty" magazines. In the United States alone, conservative estimates state there are forty million individuals each year who regularly visit porn sites, 95 percent of whom are male. The news media loves to write about the subject and it's constantly in the headlines, as shown in Figure 1.3 on the next page, because sex sells and online news outlets receive big traffic when they cover the subject.[5]

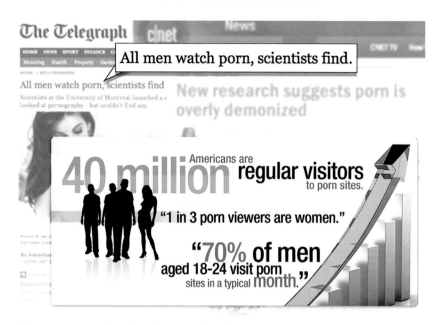

All men watch porn, scientists find.

All men watch porn, scientists find

Scientists at the University of Montreal launched a s
looked at pornography - but couldn't find any.

New research suggests porn is overly demonized

40 million Americans are regular visitors to porn sites.

"1 in 3 porn viewers are women."

"70% of men aged 18-24 visit porn sites in a typical month."

FIGURE 1.3 A selection of recent headlines and web statistics that went viral

These statistics may be both boring and overwhelming if you are currently engrossed in a struggle with your guy over pornography. There's probably even a part of you that thinks the numbers show that it's not your guy's fault, that's he's just a guy and can't control himself, that it's the adult entertainment industry's fault for seducing virtually every sexually minded man with its siren's song and its silicone parts. Even so, just for now consider that these numbers really do point to the fact that your guy is pretty much in the same boat as every other man. He is as normal as they come.

I know this knowledge probably isn't making you feel any better just yet (stay with me—hopefully that will happen later on). For now, I want to help you avoid being the type of "in denial" girlfriend or wife whom we in the adult entertainment industry often run into at social events. Let's just say that when we encounter one of these women, and when the topic of conversation comes up about what we do for a living… well, it isn't pretty. Typically, I get a knee-jerk reaction from the woman in the form of a very irritated expression on her face while her guy says something like, "Oh, that's pretty cool. But I don't really know much about the adult industry or those sites." Then, within a few minutes, when the woman finds a way to excuse herself from the conversation, the guy immediately says with an excitement akin to that of a child on Christmas morning, "That's so cool that you work for a porn company! I love that stuff! Can you get me samples or access?"

Frankly, I don't want you to be that woman. The woman who walks away, annoyed. The woman who constantly feels she has to convince her partner that he shouldn't and can't look at porn while he "agrees" and then does his best to avoid getting caught. This is important, ladies, especially when you consider the fact that if men aren't able to access pornography comfortably from their own homes, they often turn to their *workplaces*. Yes, I said they watch porn *on the job* instead of at home. I don't think I have to tell you that watching from home is a much better option than doing "you know what" on the job. What woman wants her guy to get fired for masturbating? Even at Pink Visual where we have staff who watch a lot of porn, it is also necessary for us to have a no masturbation policy at the office.

When Personal Time Impacts Professional Lives

I know, I know, it's horrifying, but it happens—and more frequently than you might think. The fact is that 20 percent of men openly admit to watching porn at work.[6] I'm sure the number is even higher if you consider the men who weren't being honest with the interviewer.

Even employees of the U.S. government are part of the trend. In July 2012 a notice went around the Missile Defense Agency from executive director John James, Jr., stating, "Specifically, there have been instances of employees and contractors accessing websites, or transmitting messages, containing **pornographic or sexually explicit images.**"[7]

If it doesn't make you see red to know that viewing porn on the job is common, the fact that government employees assigned to safeguard the security of our nation were using taxpayer dollars to do so should. James's memo went on to say, "These actions are not only unprofessional, they reflect time taken away from designated duties, are in clear violation of federal and DoD regulations, consume network resources and can compromise the security of the network through the introduction of malware or malicious code."

And it didn't just occur at the Pentagon. In 2011 twenty-eight employees of the Securities and Exchange Commission were caught looking at pornography during work hours—and none were fired. And in 2010 the superintendent of the National Parks Services resigned after being caught accessing over thirty-four hundred sexually explicit images on his work computer.

As the president of an adult studio, I agree with John James's memo. Men, watch your porn at home and not at the office. Whether you work at the Pentagon or Burger King you are accountable for the job you do. Ladies, having an open and understanding conversation about porn viewing, when ready, may even reduce the likelihood of your man making bad decisions like these at work.

These stories cover only those who were caught—either by bad luck or because they lacked the knowledge of how *not* to be caught. And that brings me to more data. Out of curiosity one day I decided to look up how many Pink Visual subscription members had registered with a .gov e-mail address. I was surprised to see that approximately one thousand members had done so. To clarify, I wasn't surprised that government workers actually look at porn on the job, but I was surprised and disappointed that they actually *used* their government e-mail address to register their subscription. Honestly, it caused me to question the intelligence of these particular government workers, especially considering how easy it is to register an e-mail address with Yahoo!, Gmail, or any other free e-mail provider. I should add that the .gov e-mails represented customers from multiple countries, but the U.S. subscriber base was at the top of the list.

Interestingly and as I previously stated, Pink Visual does have to implement a "no masturbation" policy at work. As the CEO, I don't worry half as much about our no-masturbation policy as I do about the Internet policy that we have to implement regarding social media sites such as Facebook, YouTube, and Twitter, which are huge productivity drains while people are on the clock. Funny, huh? That a porn company doesn't worry about its workers accessing porn on the job but does worry about social media.

The idea of a guy looking at porn at work does indeed sound gross, but the fact that it happens is backed up by statistical data compiled by Pink Visual and other adult entertainment companies. I have studied and digested these types of statistics for the twelve years I've been in the industry, ever since I saw that our network of websites had hundreds of thousands of daily visitors starting when we launched in 2001. At the time, we were just a small company, so I wondered about the accuracy of the data, trying to deduce if *every single* man with an Internet connection was looking at online porn. If we were getting this volume of website traffic, which continued to grow daily, what volume were the big companies, like Wicked and Vivid, generating? Pink Visual is still a small to mid-sized company, but we serve our content to over two million unique viewers per day. I tell you this, dear reader, to give you an idea of the size and scope of the marketplace and the industry. The big production houses are ten to twenty times our size, but they are doing the same thing as Pink Visual, are considered our market competitors, and are delivering content to many more millions of viewers daily.

Does Your Guy Have a Case of "The Mondays"?

While investigating these statistics early in my career, I had the opportunity to notice another interesting, yet odd, trend. On Sundays and also on Monday mornings, Internet traffic to our websites would spike and then drop off a bit throughout the week, generally picking back up on the weekends. It made sense to me that traffic on Friday, Saturday, and Sunday was high, but I wondered why Monday almost always beat out Friday and sometimes was the busiest day of the week (By the way, that same trend has continued to the present day). Because I was new to the industry I naïvely wondered, "How could so many men be taking Monday off from work in order to watch porn?" What a truly innocent statement that was!

Full realization of what was actually going on probably didn't occur to me until the first articles were published about the fact that employers were catching employees with large caches of porn on their work computers. When companies began openly discussing strategies for preventing employees from accessing X-rated material on company machines, I realized, "Oh, men are watching porn at work because their Internet connection is way faster *and* they are away from their wives."

To this day I'd like to think that men at work are just *viewing* porn, but then again I'm sure if they have a private office their activities could quite possibly entail more. And nowadays if a man has an Internet-capable mobile phone, all he needs is a private restroom and some headphones to get the job done. For sure, this insight probably isn't helping you become any more comfortable with your husband's or boyfriend's porn watching, but if he's going to do it anyhow it might be better to confront the situation directly instead of pushing him to keep this particular habit out of the house. Just think of it as a good career move.

Allow me to point out one more piece of evidence in support of the idea that all men view pornography. Even churches and religious institutions implement porn-blocking filters on their internal networks because they have experienced problems with employees and churchgoers visiting adult websites while using a Wi-Fi connection or computer belonging to the organization.[8] *Seriously.* I couldn't make this stuff up. I will be the first to admit that I find this particular lack of discretion upsetting. It's like hiding a porno magazine in a Bible while in God's house. I'm not religious, but this idea makes even me say, "Wow!"

A Few Exceptions

Of course, there are a few exceptions to the rule that "all guys look at porn," and I'll cover them here so you don't think I'm exaggerating. For instance, I'll admit that your eighty-year-old grandfather probably doesn't enjoy pornography. That is, he doesn't enjoy pornography *anymore*. However, porno magazines and posters of the classic pin-up girl were probably some of his prized possessions in WWII when he was courting your grandmother. (Don't think today's soldiers are any different; Pink Visual gets loads of correspondence from our brave men in uniform, asking if we could give them something for free.) This tendency of your family's patriarch probably didn't stop after Gram and Gramps tied the knot. In fact, it makes me think of a quote I've heard from some of my friends' grandmothers: "I don't care where he gets his appetite as long as he eats at home." Surely Grandma was referring to the strip clubs, the pin-up models, or even the XXX theatres that were around back then.

Also, to clarify, when I say "man" or "guy," I'm referring to an *actual adult*. This book isn't intended to give advice to your teenage son in his quest to access adult material. I have my own personal opinions on *that* which do not coincide with my opinions on adult men viewing porn. As a side note, however, it is interesting to point out that a recent study from the Netherlands showed that sexually explicit material actually has minimal impact on youth. Gert Martin Hald, PhD, at the University of Copenhagen, found that sexual behavior was influenced in only 0.3 to 4 percent of fifteen- to twenty-five-year-olds who watched sexually explicit material. In conclusion, Dr. Hald stated:

> *"Our data suggest that other factors such as personal dispositions— specifically sexual sensation seeking—rather than consumption of sexually explicit material may play a more important role in a range of sexual behaviors of adolescents and young adults, and that the effects of sexually explicit media on sexual behaviors in reality need to be considered in conjunction with such factors."*[9]

I think societies are in the very early stages of analyzing the data on youth and sexual material.

Now that I've clarified my position on that topic, please do me the honor of agreeing with me *just a little*. At this point you must admit that your guy watches porn—or at the very least he *really* wants to and probably feels like he is on the verge of exploding by not being able to. Again, there's a reason why you picked up this book, and it's not because you were bored; there's Sudoku for that.

As Normal as They Come

So what's wrong with him? To be blunt, the answer is: Absolutely nothing. Your man is normal and fits within the parameters of the typical sexually minded male. And the reason for his porn-viewing habits is not one that you as a woman need to be afraid of, intimidated by, or angry about. Why? Because the tendency is nothing new. Indeed, it is centuries, if not millennia, old.

Men have enjoyed visual stimulation in the form of sexually explicit images throughout history and even before. Each generation since the caveman has utilized whatever available resources they had to create such images—or what we, as an advanced civilization, might call "dirty pictures."

Think about it, girls. In Abri Castanet, in southern France, cave drawings have been found of animals, geometric figures, and—wait for it—female sex organs. Radiocarbon dating shows that they are roughly thirty-seven thousand years old. That is some very solid evidence that just like your husband or boyfriend, the men of yesteryear had sex on the brain, too. In fact, they had sex on the brain so much that they "published" their drawings, albeit in a less advanced way than we do today, on a cave wall.[10] It may be easy to laugh at the idea of comparing cave drawings of stick figures to the pornography that's available today, but both suggest that looking at certain images, whether of the human body or of watching strangers engaged in sexual action, does stimulate arousal and can lead to orgasm.

Of course, the Internet and mobile technology have made pornography more accessible than ever and fulfill a wider range of fantasies than the images discovered on cave walls in France. These leaps in technology both allowed greater access to pornography and took the medium to a new level. Nothing since the advent of the good old VHS videotape allowed for easier—and more private—access to porn. For the first time, porn didn't have to be viewed in the family room or another public area of the home, or even in the bedroom, but rather wherever one had access to a computer.

I understand, ladies, that this idea is frustrating. But let me suggest an analogy wherein women have been provided easier access to their fantasy entertainment material. Since the advent of e-readers such as the Kindle and the Nook, to name just a couple, sales of erotic novels targeted at female readers (ahem, you fans of *Fifty Shades of Grey*) have skyrocketed. Why? Because you no longer have to go into a Barnes & Noble to pick up the paperback novel with the sexy man and woman on the cover who are ready to ravage each other from the inside out. *Fifty Shades of Grey* began as an Internet sensation before it was a printed book. Originally launched as an e-book, it sold more than 250,000 copies through word-of-mouth, viral marketing before it was published in hard-copy format. This success is not unique, but it does show a trend that is increasingly marketable when dealing with erotic or sexually explicit content.[11] And that trend is based on anonymity and lack of embarrassment when purchasing—and reading—the product. Ladies, I am talking to you. Now you can now enjoy whatever erotic material turns you on without anyone knowing what you are buying and reading. A little anonymity is nice when you are indulging in fantasy and make-believe, huh? Why do you think that is any different from what your guy is doing with Internet porn? And he *is* doing it.

There is overwhelming evidence that for men, enjoying porn is the rule, not the exception. Increased accessibility via the Internet has coincided with an upsurge in "brouhaha" from wives and girlfriends who have been instructed by societal critics that men are abnormal or perverse for enjoying adult entertainment, despite the fact that it's statistically abnormal for men *not* to.

Programmed by Genetics, Shamed by Society

Most women haven't dared to evaluate the psychology behind the tendency to view pornography and the role it plays in men's lives because we've been told it isn't normal and that only men who have "something wrong" with them watch it. This societal programming comes from "experts" quoted in the news media who consider portrayals of sex—and the women who openly enjoy it, like those depicted onscreen in adult entertainment—dirty, wrong, or bad. Sometimes these messages come from authority figures like parents and religious leaders. No wonder we get so upset about the subject of pornography that we are unable to evaluate it without bias!

Think about it. As children, girls are taught that it is the chaste woman who is worthy. The woman who treats her virginity as a gift to be given away to a worthy suitor is the woman who is valued. The woman who treats her sexuality as a tool that she wields for power or dominance or even just because she likes to have sex is the harlot, the whore. We are programmed to feel that sex is something that should be done behind closed doors, that we shouldn't enjoy it and we certainly shouldn't videotape it.

Men, on the other hand, are able to freely enjoy sex without judgment. The man who acquires multiple partners and has sex openly is a "stud"; it is his genetic programming as a male that makes him want to "spread his seed." Even so, while a man's penchant for sexual activity might be dictated by genetics, society still pushes him to keep his porn-viewing habits hidden.

This rulebook we have played by has backfired. An overwhelming majority of men watch pornography, yet many feel they must lie about it. Some use incredibly poor discretion to access it outside of the home (if they live in a home with a zero-tolerance rule). Couples struggle with many different kinds of relationship problems, but wives and girlfriends often cite issues with their partner viewing pornography or claim he has an Internet porn addiction because he watches it two hours per week. (I'll tell you that two hours a week is pretty average, from the statistics we see on Pink Visual websites.) I've struggled with the entertainment form myself, and in retrospect, with all I've learned, I now realize that this is one argument most couples can avoid. Their interactions on the topic of pornography can be improved tremendously if they acquire needed information and have an open dialogue. Relationships can be hard enough without either partner creating problems that, when examined fully, are not real issues to begin with.

At the same time, I want to acknowledge that a very small minority of men do overindulge in pornography, sometimes to the point of addiction. Although it may not be a chemical addiction, porn viewing, like video games and similar entertainment, can get out of hand when it impacts someone's ability to live a normal life or be productive in society. I'm definitely not sticking up for the guy who stays in his house all day, not paying attention to his wife and kids and running up big credit card bills because his eyes are glued to a computer monitor and he has a bottle of lotion sitting on his desk. I'm serious, a porn addiction (or severe bad habit) can be just as real and damaging to one's relationship, family life, career, and finances as any alcohol or drug addiction. Addressing an addiction to porn is outside the scope of this book, which presents a model based on a "normal" level of engagement with porn. I have included a list of resources at the end of the book where you may be able to find help if you are concerned that your partner may have a compulsive or unhealthy relationship with pornography. Just as it is important for you to accept his viewing tendencies if his behavior falls within normal statistical guidelines, it is also imperative that you not live in denial if you do suspect addiction.

Personally, I think women are left with two paths to choose from. The first is to keep engaging in the same struggles, enduring the same pain and feelings of betrayal and anger every time we think about our guy looking at pornography. Or we can take the high road and step back from the situation, evaluating it more like an outsider. This involves looking into the male brain and understanding the makeup of the adult entertainment industry, and seeing if our new insights lead us to a better viewpoint and a more positive way of thinking. Taking the latter path is exactly what I did, both in my personal life and later in my professional life. It wasn't on purpose, but somehow I ended up in a career in which I had insight into the behavior not only of my guy but of virtually all men. In terms of the benefit to my marriage, I might even be tempted to call it an intervention of fate that a job in the adult industry happened to fall into my lap.

2 | My Life with Porn

I believe porn probably made my relationship with my husband a whole lot easier, as well as more positive, but like I said I didn't always have that viewpoint. It is definitely one I developed over time. When I was a teenager, like most girls my age and from my background, I didn't think about porn at all. I had no platform of knowledge about it. It was completely off my radar. In high school I'd hear the boys talk about "dirty" magazines or good R-rated movies, but I never really paid attention. I didn't have any personal interest in looking at adult pictures despite the emergence of the Internet during my formative years. Even though I had a dial-up AOL account when I was seventeen, porn for me, as well as for most girls back then, was not an issue. I can recall going to a party when I was eighteen and the guys had porn videos playing in the background. I remember thinking it was boring and immature. It was nothing more than an "eye-roll" moment. You know what I mean, ladies? That moment when you look at your friend and say, "Oh, God, guys are so dumb."

About two years later, when I was in college at the University of Arizona, I had an opportunity to think about men's relationship to porn. A guy friend of mine had recently found God and was focused on changing his ways. He stopped drinking alcohol, stopped having sex with his girlfriend, stopped masturbating, and pretty much avoided being around anyone who enjoyed a good college party. My friend must have been involved with his new way of life for around nine months when he asked to borrow my dorm-room key so he could use my computer to write a paper that was due the next day.

My friend gave me back my key later that night. I was spending the night with my boyfriend, so I hadn't yet returned to my dorm room. The next day I got an urgent call from my friend. He told me he needed to get my key again before I went back to my dorm room. He said something about having left part of his paper there, but from his demeanor and the fact that he didn't want me to return to my dorm room, I knew something was up.

We met outside my dorm. He was so upset that I didn't really care what was going on with my dorm room or computer or whatever. I just wanted to see my friend happy. He ran into the room then came back out a few minutes later, saying everything was okay. He was still shaken. Without my asking him what was up, my friend started crying and telling me that he couldn't control himself and that he had to use my computer so he could look at porn and masturbate. He said he hadn't masturbated in over six months and just could not handle it any longer. He said he had been sure he didn't leave any evidence of his actions in my dorm room, but he felt so guilty he just had to double check and, ultimately, confess.

I remember quickly and clearly telling my friend, "It's okay. It's normal. For you to go so long without doing that *isn't* normal, and you shouldn't feel guilty at all about it." My words seemed to calm him a bit, but he added that he would pray for forgiveness from God even though I made it clear that, for me, there was nothing to forgive.

My Own Personal Freak-Out

This story stands out in my head because of what I went through myself. When I later began to reevaluate how I really felt about men viewing pornography, I thought, "How could I be so open-minded and compassionate about this situation with a friend, but so rigid when it came to my guy? Was it just the fact that I created greater and possibly unachievable expectations in my head for my significant other?"

FIGURE 2.1 My Mr. Right and me as we moved him to San Antonio after his graduation in 2000

My next exposure was the one I mentioned earlier in the book, when my future husband asked me to watch porn with him and I reacted badly, crying and feeling mortified. At the time, we were in a long-distance relationship. He was in San Antonio, Texas, and I was in Tucson, Arizona, finishing up my last year in college. The plan was to visit each other every six weeks over the course of nine months.

On one of my visits to San Antonio, my guy called me into the bedroom. When I walked in, there was an adult video playing on TV and he asked me to join him in bed so we could watch it together.

From that point on everything

gets a little fuzzy in my head, but I do remember seeing two busty, naked, blonde women kissing and rubbing each other. I felt immediately stressed, and embarrassment flooded through my body as I asked him why he was watching that and how he could *ever* think I would want to watch it with him. He barely had an opportunity to respond before I started crying and yelling. It was only when I looked back on the incident that I realized he thought what he was proposing was totally innocent and simply something that might be fun for our relationship. "Fun?" I wondered. "How could pornography be fun? What does he think I am? Some sort of slut? What's more, what's wrong with him? Is he some sort of pervert?"

With tears streaming down my face, I left the room and refused to return until he turned the porn off. I remember telling him that it wasn't normal and I didn't like it. Because I was acting so furious he didn't try to fight back or present his perspective. Needless to say, it was an uncomfortable evening for both of us, and we didn't talk about porn that night or again for almost a year. I did what many women do: I swept the issue under the rug and ignored it. Even though it could be said that a big pink elephant was standing in the middle of the room, I ignored it. I pretended that the issue and my feelings about it didn't exist.

It is somewhat laughable now when I think back on the stress and angst I felt over such an innocent request, but at the time I was operating under the belief that my Mr. Right was the one guy in the world who did not look at porn. Even though he and I were separated by a thousand miles and we didn't see each other for weeks at a time, I believed he would be able to control whatever sexual urges he had, at least until we saw each other again. I really was naïve enough to believe that he was a guy who thought porn was dirty, gross, and disgusting, the way any good partner should feel about it.

How could I be so understanding toward my college friend who looked at porn in my dorm room and on my computer, yet so closed-minded about my boyfriend watching it? I believe this inner conflict is present in most women who think it is okay for all other guys to look at porn but don't want to believe that their Mr. Right is looking at it, too.

This is an important distinction to make. When it was my friend looking at Internet porn, I didn't experience feelings of low self-esteem, and I was able to avoid being stressed out by the idea of porn. My worries only reared their heads when it was *my* guy looking at porn. Clearly, my issue wasn't really with porn itself, but rather was based on my understanding of my boyfriend, his sexuality, our relationship, and my own self-confidence. Thankfully, since we were miles apart, I didn't have to evaluate those issues right away. I just enjoyed immersing myself in denying the fact that *my* guy watched porn.

Ultimately Mr. Right moved back to Tucson and we got engaged. He was perfect in many ways, and even though there was the one "situation" we'd dealt with in the past I'd convinced myself that it was a one-off and there was no way he continued to watch porn since he'd witnessed my freak-out.

Oh, the Irony

After graduating, I looked for a position in Internet marketing. I was thrilled to get a response to a job I'd applied for as an online marketing coordinator for a company called TopBucks (the precursor to Pink Visual, the company I now run). But wait…what was this? The e-mail also said they were an adult entertainment company that focused on websites and affiliate marketing. It stated that they were a professional business and didn't do film production. Although I wasn't thrilled, I needed a job. This one seemed like it would provide an opportunity to learn affiliate and web marketing, but I wasn't completely sold.

I called my fiancé and read him the e-mail. The joy in his voice was apparent as he told me to go to the interview and check it out. In his opinion money was money, and I'm sure he was imagining free passwords to the sites as a spousal benefit.

On the day of my interview I did have an "Oh my God" moment that almost made me skip the whole thing. These were the days before GPS so I had a print-out of the address, but the neighborhood was confusing. I called to let them know I was next to a 7-Eleven convenience store and asked if they could point me in the right direction. My future

FIGURE 2.2 One of the early ads for TopBucks, which eventually became Pink Visual, the company where I now serve as president

boss responded, in not-so-great English, "Ya, ya, that's us. At the back of 7-Eleven."

My heart dropped, and I told myself, no way, no how, no, no, no! I would *not* go into the back of a 7-Eleven for an interview with a porn company. I had to draw the line somewhere, and that sounded more like a backroom casting call than a job interview. I hesitated and said, "Excuse me?" When he clarified that they were in the business complex across the *street* from the back of the 7-Eleven, I felt better.

When I finally found the place, I was happy to see that it was located in a normal office building with lots of new computers and desks. There was zero porn to be seen lying around. It seemed exactly like an Internet start-up company. My future employer was in his early thirties, a computer programmer who had also graduated from the University of Arizona and worked at IBM until he started dabbling in the adult entertainment industry. Those were the days when porn images and still photos were the only things sold online because the majority of Internet connections were based on dial-up modems, which made it extremely difficult to stream video. He watched as the visitors to his ex-plicit-picture sites increased and one day decided to integrate a method to allow customers to purchase the photos instead of viewing them for free. Within two minutes he made his first sale, and a few months later he quit his full-time job to develop his own company. I had to admit I was impressed. "Now that's a story of a start-up," I thought.

I was hired on the spot. I started working the next day and became TopBucks' seventh employee and third female. It was a small office, but each person offered something different. There were graphic designers, computer programmers, and customer service staff, and although we all had different backgrounds we meshed together extremely well.

The people I worked with in the early days and the ones I work with today have had a tremendous impact on my life and my outlook. I don't know if it was the fact that we were a porno company or if it was just luck, but I have had the opportunity to work with a diverse group of people. I like to say I have been lucky, because when I was hired at age twenty-one I still had a narrow mindset. I wasn't racist or intolerant, but I definitely had a vision in my head that said everyone should be just like me: relatively mainstream, with a life partner they were planning to marry or were already married to. They would work to establish them-selves and maybe have kids down the road. I was somewhat surprised to find out that I was in the minority when it came to that life dream.

When I first started working at TopBucks, there were plenty of peo-ple who were in long-term relationships, some of which had a longer history than the one I was in. Unlike me, some had no plans to marry, and most had no desire to have kids. I also worked with people from a variety of age groups, which was a surprise and a learning experience. I figured most older people would not want to work for a porn company, but I found that what these older individuals offered the company was refreshing, often because of their sound reasoning and their experi-ence with how things were done at other businesses. This was good for our team considering that for many of us the "porn palace," as we affectionately called it, was our first real job. Even the little things like how to do employee reviews took years to figure out. I also found that

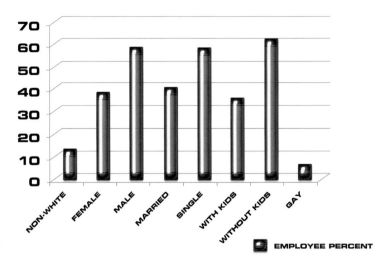

■ **FIGURE 2.3** Current demographics at the company

our company was special when it came to gay and lesbian employees. Again, I don't know if it was just dumb luck, but we offered a wonderful environment for gay and lesbian people to work in. I loved the fact that they spoke as openly about their partners and their lives as the straight employees. I loved the fact that they brought their partners to our company events and Christmas parties, and that everyone enjoyed each other's company for who they were rather than judging based on a person's sexual orientation. The diversity created a better work environment and also shaped my real-world opinions for the better.

Figure 2.3 offers a look at the demographics of the staff currently working at Pink Visual. Although we do something that is outside the realm of "normal jobs," we are pretty inclusive.

As I was writing this book, I spoke with several members of my staff, who mostly offered the same perspective. Quentin Boyer, director of public relations for Pink Visual, said, "We have a great crew—very smart, engaged young people, and I think that the company attitude makes it a great place to work. It's very laid back, but we are productive. You never feel that you are out of place because we have so many different types

FIGURE 2.4 Me with our CFO, Shelby Mowrey, and marketing director, Lea Busick, at an adult entertainment event in Las Vegas

of personalities. And it's ultimately a wonderfully flexible place. It's also great because it is a family-focused work environment. If you need time off to take care of a problem or to help a family member, there's never a question; it's always, 'You go take care of what you need to take care of.'"

I will say that working in porn does provide a lot of opportunity for "too much information" moments. These can come in many forms—from someone innocently answering a rhetorical question like, "Do people really like nipple twisting?" to staff submitting content suggestions based on their own personal interests. Hearing this stuff from a coworker is a bit different from getting suggestions from customers whom we don't know, but at the same time it has been a positive, eye-opening experience. It's not that knowing about people's sexual fetishes is really that interesting to me; rather, it has helped me realize that sexual preferences are sort of like pizza preferences. Yes, there are a lot of people who like plain pizza, but everyone's tastes vary. Some like thin crust, some like deep dish, a lot like pepperoni, and some even like anchovies. The same goes for sex. Initially my reaction was to be a little judgmental about people's sexual proclivities, but over time I began to realize that I was judging purely on the basis that others' tastes differed from mine even though their tastes didn't impact my life at all. It's not like nipple twisting was going on at the office. Slowly I began to adopt an attitude of "to each their own," and I began wondering where I even learned what was considered "normal" sex and what wasn't. This is a good question for you to ask yourself as you think about venturing into more open discussions with your guy about his porn viewing.

Even though we were a diverse team, one thing we all had in common was the realization that although we were running a business, people are more important than money. This outlook created a very good environment for work-life balance. The fact that we had a thirty-five-hour work week yet still the company seemed to be growing every day definitely helped to promote a fun and

FIGURE 2.5 An "enhanced" photo of me that my team enlarged to poster-size and hung in my office while I was on vacation

rewarding office environment. The core group of employees has always been creative, has maintained high standards, and has been known to enjoy a good practical joke or two. I share this information with you because I want to demonstrate that adult entertainment companies aren't necessarily creepy operations that function in some shadowy corporate underground. In the majority of cases they are professionally run organizations staffed by hardworking, family-oriented individuals who take pride in their work and who value a fun and supportive work environment.

"Don't Worry, Allison, Someday You Will Get a Real Job"

It was tough telling my parents that I had landed a new gig with an adult entertainment company. At first I tried to hide it from them by making up fictional company names. I told them I worked for "Cyber Tech," a name I had dreamed up. I thought that would be the end of it, but my parents were operating under the illusion that I was still their little girl and they were really curious about what I was doing with my life. Perhaps inevitably, they looked up the fictional company in the Tucson phone book and, not surprisingly, couldn't find it. Then they did an Internet search that also proved fruitless. They called to tell me what they'd found, or rather couldn't find, and to say they were concerned that I was working for some "fake" outfit that might not pay me. By this time I was out of lies—and I'm a bad liar to begin with—so I confessed that the company name was actually Cyberheat (the corporate name at the time) and that they managed various websites, including adult websites.

My mom called it "not a real job," and my father and brother laughed it off as if it weren't a valid business. I told most of my friends about the job, but I soon recognized that when meeting new people (well, mostly women), if I wanted to avoid an awkward introduction I'd better just say that I worked for an Internet hosting company. That's what I did for years because I didn't want to debate every new female acquaintance and have to defend my career choice. Because I was truly enjoying my work.

And, really, there was a lot to enjoy. My main duties consisted of contacting other websites to inquire about advertising our affiliate program, TopBucks. I learned the ropes of online advertising, negotiations via Instant Messenger, click-through ratios, and traffic analysis. I was expected to familiarize myself with our network of adult websites, which allowed me to learn about the many varieties and so-called niches that existed in the adult entertainment industry. Looking at the porn websites didn't bother me at all, although it did take some time getting used to the idea that it was totally okay to look at porn out in the open while at work. Some guys would probably say I had one of the best jobs ever, but realistically I had very little personal exposure to the sexually explicit websites. After all, I was there to do a job. I was mostly tasked with analyzing sales charts, traffic charts, and numbers in Microsoft Excel spreadsheets. And let me tell you, the data I became privy to was shocking. "Guys really pay for this stuff?" I wondered.

I couldn't believe the volume of Internet traffic that came to our network of sites, especially in light of the fact that we were still a small company and our numbers were outdoing many of the popular mainstream websites. I recall coming home during my first week on the job and telling my fiancé that after seeing the statistics from our small adult entertainment company, I realized that every man must look at pornography. My fiancé smiled at me, like he was so proud that I realized men watching porn is normal and that he, too, was normal for looking at porn. Although he didn't take advantage of my newfound openness, we began talking about porn and what drew men to it. These conversations with my fiancé were like doing research for my job. I had to understand the audience, and it was easy enough to pick my guy's brain about it. The open conversations improved our relationship and brought us closer together, which was a wonderful benefit since we were slated to get married a year later.

Within my first month of employment at TopBucks, I was happily and eagerly sharing usernames and passwords with my future husband so he could enjoy our sites and give me feedback on our product. I later learned to stop asking guys about their particular tastes when it comes to porn because each guy has specific likes and dislikes as well as opinions on what he "thinks" he likes. I have learned that pretty much every guy

FIGURE 2.6 Our wedding day in 2002

on the planet thinks that, hands down, he could direct the best porn ever, if not be the star of the best porn ever.

Although my guy and I shared opened conversations about porn and I had grown comfortable with his viewing it, I have to admit that not all of my problems were solved. I still wondered how men and women could be so different. How was it that I could easily not look at porn, but he couldn't? Why did his viewing habits still make me self-conscious and cause me to wonder somewhat about the stability of our relationship? I continued to wonder if men, including my man, wanted all women to look and act like porn stars. Of course, this train of thought caused new worries to pop into my head, such as, "Is being open about porn going to lead him to other things that I won't be so open to? What if my guy gets into something 'weird'?"

Those questions sat in the back of my mind for some time because I wasn't ready to ponder them further or deal with them openly. I was afraid of what the answers might be if I voiced my fears. For the most part, the worries weren't pressing matters, which was a good thing, because it took a few more years of working in the adult entertainment industry to find the answers. In addition, I didn't have much time to stress out about these concerns because I had a new job responsibility. This task had nothing to do with Excel spreadsheets, analyzing data, or crunching numbers. I had been assigned the project of organizing a live porn shoot at an expo event in Las Vegas.

Does This Make Me a Porn Producer?

Yes, that's right, within my first month of employment I was asked to organize a big party for our affiliates. Nothing had been planned yet besides the fact that it would include a live sex show. I thought, "How did I go from being a girl who cried a year ago when my guy wanted me to watch porn to being the organizer of a live sex show?"

Oddly enough, I had no problems with the idea of organizing the party. In fact, I loved organizing events, and that's just how I saw it, like it was any other event, but with a unique twist on the mode of entertainment. I booked the location, prepared the alcohol menu, scheduled

FIGURE 2.7 Me on the set of the photo shoot. I can't show much else from the event without earning the book an X rating. Check out the old-school Nokia cell phone.

a bartender, created the invitations, sent out the press releases—and interviewed male and female models using a little questionnaire I'd devised (see Figure 2.8 on the next page). I must say, it was the first questionnaire I'd ever written that involved the use of the word "anal."

Talking to the models pleasantly surprised me. They were all very clear about what they wanted, what they would do, and what they wouldn't do. Some only wanted to do girl/girl, most declined anal, and some only wanted to perform with their preferred male partner. The female models seemed in control of their decisions while the male models seemed extremely eager to participate. The pay was about $500 for the evening for the female models and about $200 for the guys. Each was asked to do approximately two to three scenes and commit to about five hours of work from prep time to performance. They filled out their model releases and provided copies of their driver's license or state-issued ID, showing they were over eighteen (most were over twenty). Those who were hired agreed to come back the next day for the shoot, and they all did.

Then it was show time—*live sex show time,* that is. I had come up with a proposed scene list that outlined which performers would work

The TopBucks PhotoShoot will require models to perform live sex shows with an audience watching. There can be up to 50 people watching at a time. You will need to sign the model release forms and provide 2 forms of ID and testing documentation.

Please fill out this form in order to help us match photo shoot performers.

Contact Information:
Name: _____   Phone #: _____

Availability:
Are you available to do a show on January 6th beginning at 11:30 PM?   YES   NO
Are you available to do a show on January 7th beginning at 11:30 PM?   YES   NO

Experience:
Have you ever done an adult photo shoot before? If so, how many?

_____

Have you ever done an adult video before? If so, how many?

_____

Testing:
Do you have and can you provide copies of your latest AIMS testing or other documentation for medical testing for STDs?   YES   NO

Preferences:
Please circle anything you would be willing to do during a live show:

Girl-Girl   Guy–Girl   Anal Sex   Bondage   Facial

Strip Show   Sex Toy Show   Group Sex   Other: _____

What types of toys/props would you like to use, please circle:

Anal Plug   Vibrator/Dildo   Double Dongs

Strap-Ons   Anal Beads   Penis Chin Strap

Latex Suits   Clitoral Jewelry   Edible Underwear, Liquid Latex

Police Woman Costume/Handcuffs   Nurse Costume/Self-Examiner

Whipped Cream, Food Products (i.e., bananas)

Bondage Equipment (whips, paddles, rope, nipple clamps, ball gag, etc.)

Other: _____

Payment:
Each photo shoot will require you to be at the show for about 5 hours. You could be asked to perform anything from 2 to 4 shows (each about 25 minutes long). How much would you prefer to be paid $_____?

■ FIGURE 2.8 The model questionnaire used for our live photo shoot party

together and in what order, but the list ultimately became useless. The event was held in a huge hotel suite that had a large attached bedroom. The audience was kept out of the bedroom until show time, and I hung out backstage until everything was ready. The event involved more nakedness than I had ever seen in my life. I also noticed that everyone was very comfortable with it and with what they were doing, no matter if they were having actual sex, or if they were doing a normal activity like brushing their hair, albeit naked, with eight other people in the immediate vicinity going about their business.

I opened the bedroom doors and announced that the first scene was about to start. At that moment the event switched from a party of geeky webmasters to what could only be described as a paparazzi convention. A flood of dudes came in all at once with camera flashes popping. They were all so excited.

The first scene featured two women who rolled around on the bed together and gave the audience a great show. Then it was time for the second scene to commence, this one featuring a man and a woman. The couple came out strong, but soon there was a hiccup. The guy was having performance anxiety. He'd been okay in the bathroom as he was prepping for the scene, but as soon as he entered the bedroom and saw all those other guys he just couldn't get the job done. The female star did her best to "inspire" him, but to no avail. I called for a break and asked the audience to step outside.

I asked the other guys if they could go on. One by one, each of them began doubting himself and bowing out. Feeling frantic, and realizing I had no other options, I decided, what the hell, let's ask the partygoers if they are interested in participating. I walked around the group and propositioned guys, for lack of a better word, asking them if they wanted to be in a scene. I thought it would be a dream come true for some of them. Most of them were single and had probably never even dated a woman as sexy as some of the female models who were involved in the event. But out of the two hundred or so guests, not a single man was willing to volunteer. A few joked about it and started to make their way to the bedroom, but quickly reconsidered and opted out.

Ultimately, the scene list was tossed and the show continued, focusing only on "girl-girl" scenes. The audience loved it and in fact was probably happier because they didn't have to see any penises. My boss was pleased with the job I did. I walked away having learned that although men may believe that being a porn star and having sex with hot women all day seems like a great job, when it comes down to it very few are able to act on the fantasy because, really, it's hard work. (Forgive the pun.)

Meeting Porn Stars

At this point, ladies, I suppose you are dying for me to address what the girls are like. I get into the subject of "porn stars" later in the book, including addressing the mythology and misconceptions that surround them, but for now I will say that my work on the live event in Las Vegas led me to realize that the female performers in the adult industry are more-than-willing participants when it comes to acting on set.

The women I met were extremely comfortable with their bodies and their sexuality. And let me tell you, no one was forcing or coercing them to do this; these women actually enjoyed doing the adult scenes. As with any profession, there are different reasons why individuals end up pursuing one job over another. Some of the women at the event seemed like they were doing it for the attention and to be present at the party, while others made it clear that their career choice was helping them pay for their college tuition.

The women showed up sober and levelheaded and wanted to do their job well. I know all this because I was the one who hired them. I felt so uncomfortable about interviewing them out loud that instead I had them circle "yes" or "no" in response to the question, "Would you like to participate as an adult performer in our live sex show?"

After the convention, business continued to boom. My boss was happy with my performance and eventually increased my responsibilities, promoting me to marketing director. Soon thereafter, we bumped up our staff—there were now twenty-one of us—and I hired an assistant to do the tasks I'd initially been hired to do. Morale was high. It seemed like anything we touched, anything we were involved in, anything we innovated turned to solid adult entertainment gold.

The Times They Are a-Changin'

I'm assuming that most of you probably aren't familiar with my company or our products. That's totally okay because to be honest, we're not a huge company or even a well-known brand amongst porn viewers. Yes, we have some decent brand recognition, but we're not *Hustler* or *Playboy*. However, I do think our company is pretty special, and everything I have experienced during my employment with Pink Visual has shaped my ideas about porn and its relationship to both women and men. I think without some of this information, you may be inclined to believe that the management at adult companies sits around talking about how they know all of the negative consequences associated with their products, but like the tobacco or alcohol industries, wants to cover them up to make more sales. Please believe me when I say that it's nothing like that or for sure I would have been out the door long ago. Let me explain what happened next for me and Pink Visual.

As we continued to launch more websites, we began to realize that in order to grow our company and secure our brand in the marketplace, we needed to produce our own content instead of simply purchasing it from others. Especially in the adult entertainment sector, offering original content helps a company stand on its own in the digital age, when business models are quickly copied or imitated and competition appears suddenly and unexpectedly. In addition, content production allows for a more personal relationship with the consumer, who is able to provide feedback on what they enjoy and what they would like to see more of.

Initially, the idea of producing our own content scared me a bit. I imagined that our office would be full of porn stars and worried about how that might interrupt our workflow. As it turned out, production occurred in Los Angeles; we edited the footage and processed it for use on the Web. Every time we launched a new website, sales immediately surged, a trend that continued into 2005.

By then I had been promoted to vice president of operations. I coordinated new website launches and new product branding and promotion. We were attempting to diversify our product base, but our bread and butter was still the adult websites and affiliate programming that attracted online marketers to sell our products.

As VP of ops, I was asked to attend the consumer tradeshows that serve as a rallying point for industry members and a way to interact with fans. The shows are great because they provide a chance to get your products as well as your stars out there and to build some brand loyalty. The biggest consumer show is the Adult Entertainment Expo, sponsored by *Adult Video News* (AVN), a trade publication for the industry. The show is held every January in Las Vegas and coincides with the annual awards show (yes, we have an awards show, and I can assure you the Oscars have nothing on the AVN Awards). Frankly, the Adult Entertainment Expo is, and probably always will be, a circus. Men (and in recent years an increasing number of women) young and old, true fans as well as the simply curious, wander around with joyous smiles on their faces while collecting every available freebie and interacting with their favorite stars.

Standing at the shows all day killed my feet, but being there certainly upped my self-confidence because a few of the male attendees would point to a picture of a beautiful porn star showcased in our booth and ask if it was me. It was flattering yet also bewildering since I was usually clad in a business suit. One year I was six months pregnant and showing. I took the comments as a compliment, although my coworkers would tease me by making up porn-movie titles like *Alli Does Austin*.

Although the business remained fun and exciting, the market atmosphere was growing tougher. We saw more competitors entering, and ultimately saturating, the market, and it became almost a daily occurrence that a company launched a new website, attracting affiliates away from us and over to them. Still, Pink Visual, which is the company name we transitioned to in 2004, was holding its own as the result of a lot of hard work, dedication, and commitment to innovation.

At the end of 2006 I was promoted to president, which entailed overseeing all 120+ employees. We were shooting close to forty scenes a month out of production studios in Los Angeles and other countries. As president, most of my duties remain similar to those of my original position as online marketing coordinator, but with a broader viewpoint. A typical day consists of answering e-mails, reviewing membership and traffic statistics, and going through financial reports. I aim to ensure that our path and future remain clear, a task that has its challenges considering the rocky road the adult entertainment industry has been on since 2006.

Digital piracy in the adult entertainment sector was teaching our consumer that there was no need to purchase our once highly valued products. The market was becoming oversaturated because the barrier to producing adult content was more or less nonexistent. Almost anyone could create an adult network and begin driving traffic in very little time. Moreover, the home computer was becoming the family computer and a source for other forms of entertainment like Facebook, blogs, YouTube, etc. That meant less private computer time for the man of the house. To top it all off the economy was in decline. The era of easily turning adult entertainment into gold was coming to an end. Pink Visual suffered declines in revenue despite many attempts to change our offerings—until 2007 when the first iPhone was released.

Pink Visual was one of the first companies to develop an XXX website for the iPhone. We sort of had to go about it through the back door. Apple is very strict about what they want and do not want on their devices. Porn happens to fall into the "do not want" category. I've had daydreams that Apple would simply acquiesce and create an adult-verified section within their app store, but a couple of years ago Steve Jobs made it very clear that this wasn't going to happen anytime soon. Pink Visual had to figure out a way around the "Apple barrier." After much brainstorming and some trial and error—including developing an app that featured something as innocent as women in lingerie and which was pulled down within a few months—our talented software developers designed a mobile website for use on the iPhone that looks and feels like an app. Slowly we started seeing mobile traffic increase to the site, so we focused on what worked, launching more mobile websites and developing them to function on multiple devices.

We've received industry awards for "Best Mobile Company," and I was the recipient of Xbiz's Woman of the Year and the Free Speech Coalition's Leadership Award. I was listed by CNBC.com in a feature on "Power Brokers of the Adult Industry" and recognized by BigThink .com on their list of "Top Ten Women in Male Dominated Fields." Ironically enough, I was also selected for Newt Gingrich's 527 Advisory Council as an Entrepreneur of the Year, an appointment that was

FIGURE 2.9 With our sales director (and also good friend), Kristin Wynters, at the Xbiz Awards in 2011

rescinded after they realized I run an adult entertainment company. The publicity highlight of my career grew from that debacle when I was honored as one of Keith Olbermann's "World's Best Persons" on his MSNBC show *Countdown.* I'm still waiting to someday be invited to appear on *The Daily Show,* which stars one of my celebrity crushes, Jon Stewart. We at Pink Visual take pride in the fact that we managed to carve a good solid couple of years out of the hard times despite the fact that many of our colleagues in the industry went out of business.

Unfortunately, the piracy issue began to reappear in late 2011, impacting consumer demand and putting our company behind the eight ball once again as we figure out how to prevent further loss.

Pink Visual Today

The company is now in the middle of a complicated dichotomy. There are more people viewing online porn today than ever before, yet fewer of them are willing to pay for it because they've been exposed to so much of it for free. Furthermore, many people fear giving their credit card information to an adult entertainment company, a concern that is partially valid as some bad apples in the industry have taken advantage of customers through creative billing and credit card scams.

Although the piracy issues in porn have been compared to those in the music industry, the problems afflicting the adult industry are unique. Let's say you are searching for a song by Taylor Swift. If you can't find it for free online you probably won't be satisfied instead with a song by Katy Perry. The two artists aren't interchangeable. Ultimately, you will probably buy the Taylor Swift song. With adult content, that isn't the case. If a guy is surfing the Internet for some free porn, maybe even looking for a favorite star, if he can't find her it's safe to say he can probably find something else that will achieve the same result. Unlike music, our product is interchangeable, which is why piracy has hurt our business, even as the music business has figured out a way to work with online music sharing and downloads.

I believe the adult industry is the business most impacted by digital piracy. My company has been heavily involved with the antipiracy movement. Moreover, I believe in the power of litigation because we deem that we are on the right side of the law. We have dealt with the problem in ways that have contributed to our ability to remain in business, including starting an antipiracy company that services multiple industries, both inside and outside the adult entertainment sector. But it's a rocky road out there. Who would have thought that my career in porn would evolve in such a way that I would also be operating an antipiracy organization that helps both mainstream and adult companies?

I've witnessed many of the biggest and most profitable production companies close their doors. Others, like ours, have reduced production schedules by nearly 70 percent. The condition of the market leads me to wonder if the consumer will become unhappy with the limited number of videos being produced and eventually become willing to pay for new content. Or will it go the other way, with the consumer settling for less because it's free?

The future of pornography in recorded picture and video format, such as DVDs and videotapes, is very much up in the air. But one thing is true for sure: Pornography in some form will continue to exist, as it has throughout history.

3 | Porn — Past and Present

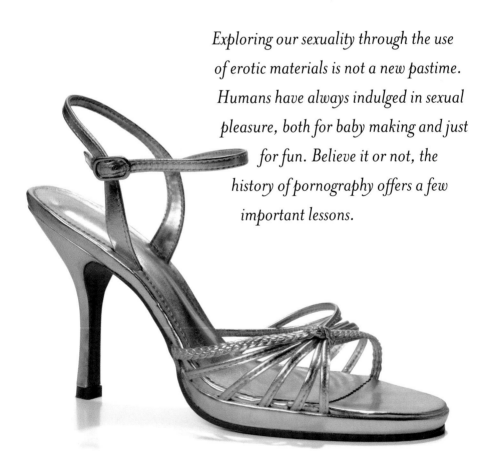

Exploring our sexuality through the use of erotic materials is not a new pastime. Humans have always indulged in sexual pleasure, both for baby making and just for fun. Believe it or not, the history of pornography offers a few important lessons.

First, although many people would like to consider pornography a new issue facing men, women, relationships, and society, it is not. Second, pornography production has steadily increased through every generation, even during eras when the topics of sex and sexuality were repressed and shunned by "polite" members of society. Finally, men's attraction to pornography is very deeply rooted in the male brain at a level of programming that can't simply be turned off by a wife or girlfriend who complains about it.

Early Erotica

Let's look at the earliest evidence of "pornography." As I alluded to in the last chapter, the first sexually explicit depictions, cave etchings that feature female and male body parts, date from over thirty-five thousand years ago. Some scholars believe they were drawn purely for the purpose of art, but others theorize they were meant to arouse sexuality.

There is less controversy around the purpose of the thirty-thousand-year-old siltstone phallus found in Germany in 2010. Researchers say this dual-purpose tool was used both as a flint to ignite fires and as a sex toy.[1] That seems like a lot of effort to put into a sex toy, in my opinion, but it clearly demonstrates the human drive for sexual pleasure even in the early ages. Similar artifacts clearly shaped like penises that have been carved from stone, bone, and metals have been found that date back to 6,000 BC or earlier, and these objects are associated with a wide range of cultures from the ancient Greeks to the ancient Chinese.

Also interesting is *how* we interpret these explicit artifacts and drawings based on whether they depict a man or a woman. For the most part, archaeologists describe ancient representations of nude males as portraying gods, hunters, or warriors. By contrast, explicit drawings of women are often considered prehistoric pornography. Why can't the opposite be true? Maybe the drawings featuring women symbolized goddesses, mothers, wives, or shamans. Maybe the drawings of men were meant as erotica—for either men or women. In any case, male archaeologists' assumptions that a stick figure with a triangle for a vagina is pornographic show how readily many men's brains seem to go in that direction. I'm not the only one who's noticed this bias. Blogger and author Violet Socks raises the possibility that prehistoric artifacts of nude women may have depicted natural processes such as childbirth. She writes, "The archaeologist assumes the artist who created the figurine was male; why? He assumes the motive was lust; why? Because that's all he knows. To his mind, the image of a naked woman with big breasts and exposed vulva can only mean one thing: porn! Porn made by men, for men! And so he assumes, without questioning his assumptions, that the image must have meant the same thing 35,000 years ago. No other mental categories for 'naked woman' are available to him. His mind is a closed box."[2]

My theory is that thirty-five thousand years ago, and in many eras since, naked and sexualized forms of men and women have been used *both* as art *and* for purposes of arousal. The two did not always have to be separated because many cultures accepted sex as a natural, even artistic, expression of the body. Sex wasn't always the taboo subject it is today. Consider an artistic masterpiece such as Michelangelo's painting *Leda and the Swan,* which was based on a Greek myth and depicts a nude Leda being seduced, or raped, by the god Zeus in the form of a swan (see Figure 3.1).

Similarly, within ancient Greek and Roman societies there was no concept of pornography; sexually explicit art was simply viewed as depicting daily life. The Greeks and Romans produced works of art exhibiting standard heterosexual bedroom behavior as well as homoerotic works like Sappho's *Hymn to Aphrodite,* a poem describing lesbian eroticism. When viewing artifacts from ancient Greece, it is almost *more* difficult to find art without sexual references or nudity.[3] Check out the earthenware wine cup in Figure 3.2. The erotic scene depicted on its rim doesn't leave much to the imagination. Obviously, it wasn't the modern adult entertainment industry that invented the idea of a *ménage à trois* or an orgy.

Similar types of sexual imagery occur in artifacts from Asia, South America, and other parts of Europe. I was surprised, although maybe I shouldn't have been, to run across sex toys and pornographic sculptures

FIGURE 3.1 Drawing by Cornelius Bos of the lost original by Michelangelo from the 1500s (currently on display at the British Museum in London)

FIGURE 3.2 Erotic scene from 510 BC (Marie-Lan Nguyen/Wikimedia Commons)

FIGURE 3.3 Me posing with a dildo sculpted out of wood found at store near Chichen-Itza in Mexico

when visiting the ancient Mayan region of Chichen-Itza, Mexico, in 2003. Although these are present-day creations from the local Mayan people, the objects reflect their history. Here I am holding a wooden sculpted dildo with balls and all (see Figure 3.3). It didn't vibrate, but the craftsmanship was impeccable.

Figure 3.4 shows mini sculptures portraying many sexual positions. We can probably conclude that the Mayans, a highly developed early culture, weren't having a bunch of boring sex.

I'll stop with my vacation photos and get back to discussing the history of porn. As mentioned,

FIGURE 3.4 Another odd vacation find at the same store near Chichen-Itza

explicit depictions have existed since humans realized sex could be used not only for reproductive purposes but also for fun and entertainment—so, basically, since the beginning of time. Although many cultures were open-minded when it came to sex, there have been periods throughout history when societal norms dictated conservative behavior, sex was demonized, and individuals or mediums deemed "sexual" were repressed and shunned.

Protecting the People from Themselves

Makers of pornography or sexually explicit materials have existed on the fringes of society for ages. In the 1700s authors of novels considered "erotic" or "sexual" were vilified, called deviants or depraved, and ultimately prosecuted, their books banned. Other artists endured controversy for their nude and erotic depictions, including the nineteenth-century French painter Édouard Manet. Manet was one of the first artists dedicated to approaching modern subjects and real-life situations. He became a pivotal figure as the art world transitioned from Realism to Impressionism. One of his early paintings, *Olympia,* garnered great controversy for depicting a nude prostitute. Interestingly, the word "pornography" is derived from the Greek words *porni,* meaning prostitute, and *graphein,* to write.[4]

Although what constitutes pornography is subjective, we have the Victorians to thank for modern interpretations and opinions regarding the work. During the 1800s the first laws were created prohibiting certain transactions regarding pornography or people's exposure or access to the medium. Still, production and distribution of pornography continued, and people in suppressed cultures were able to find it.

The act of suppressing natural human tendencies continues in many cultures today in which pornography is completely illegal. Whereas the sale of hardcore pornography is legal in the United States and Canada, its influence in other areas of the world is controversial. Certain countries—including Belarus, Iceland, South Korea, China, Malaysia, and the majority of Middle Eastern countries—have laws on the books outlawing the production, sale, import, distribution, and viewing of pornographic materials, even for adults. In some cases violation of these laws is punishable with prison time.

The reason given for preventing the general public from accessing pornography usually has to do with "preserving morals." The Palestinian Islamist organization that governs the Gaza strip, Hamas, has recently instituted new Internet censorship rules, including blocking access to any pornographic website. Osama Al-Eisawi, minister of communication and information technology for Hamas, stated, "Our social fabric needs protection and we are actually protecting Internet users in Gaza."[5] At the same time, it is important to note that Pink Visual's web statistics show that citizens of societies in which access to porn is restricted or outlawed still manage to retrieve sexually explicit websites in an overrepresented way considering the limitations imposed on them by their governments (see Figure 3.5).

Probably one of the most noteworthy ironies of the religious-based antiporn mentality is the story of the porn stash found at Osama Bin Laden's hideout. Despite the fact that the house did not have Internet or any other hard-wired communication, an extensive collection of modern, prerecorded pornography was found. In fact, officials familiar with similar confiscations have said that the discovery of pornography is not uncommon in such cases. The hypocrisy is evident here.

As is the case with most banned materials, repression has failed to prevent citizens from viewing erotica and pornography. And there have always been innovators eager to integrate pornography into any new technologies. Soon after Louis Daguerre invented the first practical photography process, in 1835, photos of nude and pornographic images were being taken that required models to sit without moving for several minutes. The main audience for these expensive photos were rich people, who were the only ones who could afford them. During that time period, folks of lesser socioeconomic means enjoyed nude and erotic photography using stereoscopes, which use offset images viewed separately and simultaneously by the left and right eye of the viewer to create the illusion of three-dimensional depth.[6] Pornographic films were produced soon after the invention of the film process in 1895. One

FIGURE 3.5 Statistics of Internet visitors from some non-porn-friendly countries to Pink Visual sites. Canada is used for comparison sake. (Source: Pink Visual Internal Data)

of the most famous is "Le Coucher de la Mariée," which was directed by Albert Kirchner. Shot in 1896 (that didn't take long, huh?), the film featured a seven-minute striptease performed by Louise Willy.[7]

Although by today's standards much of the work produced during the nineteenth century would be considered pretty tame, the fact is there were many early pornography pioneers throughout the world. Unfortunately, in most cases their work did not survive, and we are left with only written evidence of their existence. One such organization is the Saturn-Film production company (not to be confused with Saturn Films, the present-day production company owned by American actor

Nicolas Cage). Saturn-Film company, owned by Austrian photographer and pioneer film producer Johann Schwarzer, produced about fifty-two erotic movies between 1906 and 1911. They were featured on men-only theatre nights in Austria. It was the first company of its kind based in Austria and was run along the lines of a public company. Schwarzer wanted to market his films to the general public; he didn't believe that his material should be shunned simply because it contained nude female forms and themes of voyeurism. He advertised his films in newspapers, in trade journals, and through other means. He proudly featured his logo in his advertisements, just like any other European film producer.

After experiencing some early success, the organization was the victim of a police raid in Vienna when the government issued a declaration expressing the need for a crackdown against erotic work. During the raid, authorities destroyed the main vault housing the film archive, effectively shutting the company down. Neither Schwarzer nor the company ever recovered. Although Schwarzer tried to regain his reputation in the film-distribution industry, he was unable to. He was killed during World War I while on active duty. Clips from a few of his films still exist.[8]

What I find especially distressing in the story of the Saturn-Film company is the fact that the censors didn't stop at shutting down the operation but also destroyed the films, which were then gone forever. No doubt my strong commitment to freedom of expression has been partly shaped by the relatively open era in which I live, but I recognize the priceless legacy behind the materials destroyed in those raids, whether or not they can be considered "art." The idea of a destructive form of censorship should be upsetting to any individual who values freedom of expression, whether or not she or he is a proponent of adult entertainment.

Going Mainstream

Trends around erotica steadily evolved. As technology and distribution models improved, so did the interest in this form of entertainment.

During the 1920s, silent erotic films were screened in brothels, and magazines featuring nude women made their way to a wider network of customers. As film became more popular and widespread and methods of printing improved, enterprising individuals behind early-twentieth-century erotica were intent on figuring out how to utilize these methods to sell their wares. So-called "stag" films became popular with travelling salesmen in the 1940s. "Pin-up girl" posters piqued interest in erotica as a form of entertainment. The pin-up girl was not an early version of the porn star; rarely did the women in the posters "take it all off." They had careers as fashion or glamour models, actresses, or dancers, and the mass-produced images were intended to promote their careers. Of course, some very popular actresses and models were also famous pin-up girls, including Betty Grable, Lauren Bacall, Bette Davis, and even "Dorothy" herself, Judy Garland. By the 1950s, photos of the female form became increasingly risqué, shifting the focus from the celebrity's legs to her breasts. Hugh Hefner purchased photos of Marilyn Monroe to use in the inaugural issue of *Playboy*, in December 1953. Needless to say, Norma Jean is probably the world's most famous and emulated pin-up girl.

The 1950s also brought photography to the amateur with the invention of the 8mm camera, allowing producers of erotica to supply the market's demand. Entrepreneurs like Harrison Marks, from Britain, and Lasse Braun, from Italy, created lucrative careers out of shooting erotic films and pornography.[9] This may have been the official start of the popular amateur porn trend, which featured lesser-known women whose bodies and faces looked "real."

In the 1960s, as positive attitudes toward sexuality and the human form grew, countries like Denmark and the Netherlands abolished their laws prohibiting pornography in all forms, whether "soft-" or "hardcore." Legal victories for producers of erotica and pornography followed. After the state of Massachusetts banned the Swedish film *I Am Curious (Yellow)* for its scenes depicting sexual intercourse, the United States Supreme Court ultimately ruled that the film could be screened in Boston theatres since neither children nor an "unwilling public" would be exposed to the material.[10] This particular case didn't modify obscenity standards in U.S. law, but it did pave the way for laws that administer and regulate the adult entertainment industry today.

The 1970s saw movement in the United States toward what would become today's industry trends. Adult-specific movie theatres opened that featured films such as *Mona the Virgin Nymph* as well as classics like *Deep Throat, The Devil in Miss Jones,* and *Behind the Green Door.* Further critical acclaim and acceptance was won when mainstream movie theatres screened these films for mixed, and nonmasturbatory, audiences.

It is important to understand that until the 1970s many of the laws that regulated (or didn't regulate) the industry led to considerable legal discord as they dealt with the emergence of pornography among mainstream consumer factions. The decade established rather "fuzzy" legal logic to determine what types of pornography were obscene and what types were not. The 1973 Supreme Court case *Miller v. California* established the so-called "Miller Test" for determining what was considered "obscene." The test, which is still used today, is based on three questions that consider opinion and ambiguous measures in determining whether a medium—be it film, photo, or written text—is obscene. Distribution of material could be halted if all three of the following criteria received "yes" answers:

1. whether "the average person, applying contemporary community standards" would find that the work, taken as a whole, appeals to a "prurient" interest in sex
2. whether the work depicts or describes, in a patently offensive way, sexual conduct specifically prohibited in a state's law
3. whether the work, taken as a whole, lacks serious literary, artistic, political, or scientific value[11]

The test is widely criticized by both professionals in the adult entertainment industry and proponents of free speech. To the layperson, the parameters of the Miller test might not seem like a big deal, but please consider this: because the test establishes no straightforward definition of what is and is not obscene, it allows for subjective interpretation. It also introduces the pesky term "community standards" into the mix.

Let's say Person A, who lives in Texas, happens to love downloading and watching threesomes. The material itself is created and produced in California, which, it could be argued, is a liberal area of the country and might be more open-minded toward what is considered adult entertainment. However, in Texas, the environment is arguably not so liberal, and maybe some district attorney there who finds the idea of a threesome obscene and despicable is looking to make an example of the industry and its presumed ability to degrade citizens' minds. The D.A. decides to go after the video producers for distributing their products in Texas, even though they are located in California and the products were bought by an adult for use in a private environment. This scenario may sound far-fetched, but believe it or not it could happen—some district attorney, if he or she really wanted to get down and dirty, could go after the pornographer in this situation simply because the D.A. defined threesomes as obscene.

If you think this hasn't happened you would be wrong. The legal doctrine of "community standards" has become significantly challenging to deal with because of the ease of distribution allowed by the Internet. Just because some variation on adult entertainment might be viewed as acceptable in New York City or Los Angeles doesn't mean it would be in Birmingham, Alabama. I'm providing this background so you can understand that we in the adult industry are dealing with a legal system that is not only increasingly out of touch but also based solely on the very subjective "eye of the beholder."

The 1980s saw two important developments: The production of porn became legal in California, and producers of adult entertainment began to shoot on videotape. They recognized that the new technology permitted consumers to access erotic material in the privacy of their own homes. Because videotape was less expensive than film, and because the medium released the individual from the stigma associated with having to walk into an adult theatre, the market opened up significantly, leading to exponential growth. This was the first natural shift in the market driven by American men who wanted to watch porn privately. The move brought more producers into the industry, driving an increase in the variety of pornography created to suit varying tastes, which in turn expanded the audience even more.

In the 1990s DVDs were introduced, which provided higher quality for the home theater. But it was the Internet that truly brought pornography to the privacy of the home in a way that video and DVD never could. While videotape might have made it possible for the average consumer to view pornography at home, he still had to procure the videotape, whether it was via mail order (risking possible judgment by the postal carrier) or by going to a video store. With the advent of the Internet the average guy with a reliable connection no longer had to walk into an adult store or purchase magazines from the local convenience store and risk an awkward experience, like running into his boss or neighbor. This increased accessibility and created familiarity.

The "porn star" also emerged in the 1990s. I am pretty sure anyone reading this book can name at least one porn star, for example Jenna Jameson, arguably the most famous of the '90s. The Internet prompted porn stars' rise to fame and created their enduring place in American culture. The female porn star, whether celebrated or demonized, is part of the reason why pornography has gone mainstream. Love her or hate her, she not only fascinates but has become a symbol—for some representing the downfall of our culture, for others female sexual empowerment.

Familiarity Breeds Disapproval

Now we have porn produced in high definition (although not always delivered in HD) and available via streaming video on computers, Internet-capable TVs, and mobile devices. Porn is, to the chagrin of some, everywhere. The modern adult industry pushes to make its products higher quality, more accessible, more private—and more innovative. Some of the adult flicks produced in 3D have been huge hits, which hints at the possibility of where porn could go next. As in previous eras, the adult industry, even during economic slow periods, has remained quick to take advantage of new technologies that can improve production and delivery. This agility will ensure the continued growth of viewership.

There is no denying that the industry in recent years has experienced exponential growth in interest and access to our products. On the flip side, along with that growth we have seen a more passionate and outspoken antiporn movement based on objections ranging from the religious to the feminist to the political. Pornography and antipornography cultures have clashed, generating deep and passionate emotion on all sides. The controversy has turned pornography into the dirty secret every man enjoys. Both consumers of adult entertainment and industry members are surrounded by this shame-filled environment, and our opportunity to be heard by our critics has been reduced and silenced. You may think that I'm exaggerating here, but let me give some examples. One is that often adult companies want to show how professionally they are run and want to share publicly their preferred vendors. Whenever that is attempted, most mainstream vendors say, "no thank you, please don't reference our name with your business," but they will be definitely there to send you a bill for using their services. Not the biggest deal in the world there, but an example of how we rarely have the opportunity to share how legitimate we are because our mainstream counterparts are afraid of what porn critics think.

There's also example after example of nonprofit groups who are willing to accept donations from adult companies as long as it's not public knowledge. Once the public becomes aware of it, they often decline the donation. My point here, is that we have very little opportunity to show the public who we really are. And of course, the bigger deal is the government. Unlike every other industry who lobbies for revenue increasing legislation, there's not a Senator or a Congressman who's willing to stand up for the porn industry since for sure it will end his career. The irony there is that honestly a lot of adult companies would support some level of formal adult verification for viewing as long as it was enforced consistently.

Obviously, given the statistics, this means that there are a lot of hypocrites out there who really enjoy adult entertainment, but don't want anyone to know. This "perfect storm" of increased demand and heightened opposition was one of my inspirations for writing this book.

I hope that "pulling back the veil," so to speak, will help to accurately represent our industry to the general public and to the naysayers who are quick to point out our flaws while ignoring the positive aspects of our business. The double standards displayed by many of our critics have always been a huge pet peeve of mine. Even the tobacco industry has had an opportunity to present its case to its critics and to the U.S. government. At least the adult entertainment industry has never knowingly poisoned the health of American consumers for profit.

I have always wondered why this contradictory state of affairs exists in the nation that is supposed to be the most free and open-minded on the planet. Even if you were to believe every false statement made by a critic of the adult entertainment industry, the damage they say we do doesn't come close to that perpetuated by other industries that knowingly distribute products they recognize could be fatal to their consumers. So why has the industry promoting sex and sexuality been told to keep to ourselves and not be seen with others in public?

Many studies, including the one conducted by the University of Montreal that I mentioned earlier, show that pornography does not create the negative impact many of its critics claim it does. Our products are not a springboard for perverted or deviant behavior, and we in the industry actively reject the exploitation of children and avoid engaging in unsafe or risky practices. If anything, my industry has policed itself, implementing policies and procedures that benefit all involved, from the models onscreen to the consumers at home.

The University of Montreal study noted that all of the participants stated that they support gender equality and that their perceptions of women have not changed based on their pornography-viewing habits.[12] Even present-day feminists are beginning to recognize that it is within a woman's right to choose to be in adult films and to depict the full range of female sexuality. Additional controversial research (controversial due to the subject, not the results) shows that an increased accessibility to pornography reduces instances of rape. When access to pornography is up, rape is down, as are other sexual crimes, proving that pornography does not increase men's aggression toward women.

Still, even though the data support the idea that, at a minimum, pornography isn't all bad, it's far from being widely accepted.

A glimmer of hope exists due to the younger generation's more accepting views of pornography. Younger women grew up being privy to their male counterparts' opinions and views regarding online porn. Moreover, many young women have affirmed that they themselves viewed the medium as teenagers because they were curious about it and wanted to know what the fuss was about. Even though the up-and-coming generation easily accepts that most men view porn and there's probably not much that can be done about it, this doesn't resolve all the problems related to women, men, and pornography. Awareness needs to continue to grow among people of all ages; we can't just sit by and wait until today's twenty-somethings are in charge of running things. Plus, this is about sex and there is a mature conversation that needs to be had among mature adults who have the necessary experience so we don't turn the discussion into what might be considered an eighteen-year-old's version of sex—"Yes, boobs everywhere, please." Many men and women still have the insecurities around porn that have plagued previous generations, including my own Gen Xers. And it's still far too easy to recruit both men and women to the antiporn point-of-view—at least publicly, even if they enjoy viewing porn themselves in the privacy of their bedrooms.

4 | Who Taught Us to Hate Porn Anyway?

Let me state up front that there's not one single person,
circumstance, or group that has encouraged women
to hate pornography. If only finding a culprit
were that simple. I sure don't remember having
an awkward conversation with my parents in
which they told me that images and videos
of men and women engaging in sex acts
were unacceptable or wrong. I don't
even recall its being mentioned in
the church I went to as a child.

Even with all the girl talk I've engaged in over the years, there was not one single conversation where someone told me porn was horrible or suggestive of sexual deviance or mental instability. So how did I come to hate the fact that my guy watched porn when I was hit with that reality? Was I in a complete fantasyland, thinking my guy would have eyes only for me and wasn't remotely attracted to porn? Based upon my reaction, maybe that's what I thought.

I've pondered these questions over the years. I've brainstormed with my girlfriends about their own experiences. I've concluded there are three things that have contributed to us girls disliking porn. One is a natural difference between how women's and men's brains operate; the second is parental (and, by extension, societal) overprotection; and the third is the actual content of most porn. Let's look at each of these factors.

Nature: Men vs. Women

Actual proof exists to show that women's brains function differently from men's brains, even when it comes to sexual arousal. This is probably pretty obvious when you think about the anecdotal evidence, like the fact that most men are always "in the mood" while most women are more inclined to "have a headache." Or consider the fact that men have a lot more surface area to cover when it comes to physical arousal. Compare the penis to the clitoris or the fabled G-spot. Yes, God gave us women a "spot" for arousal, but he/she/it provided our guys a whole "stick" to play around with. Beyond the anecdotal evidence is the fact that the portion of the brain that regulates sexual behavior, the amygdala, is significantly larger in men than in women. I'll get more into the science of the sexual brain in the next chapter.

Yes, men are naturally more drawn to all things sexual, but something else contributes to men's fascination with porn. Huge quantities of evidence show that, for the most part, men's brains prefer instant gratification and women's brains want to ensure long-term payoff. This has been discovered in studies regarding, of all things, shopping: Men buy items to fill an immediate need while women purchase with longer-term needs in mind. When I first encountered this research I thought of all my female friends who had complained at one time or another about sending their husbands to do the grocery shopping. The wives had to return to the store the next day to get items that were meant to restock household inventory, such as cleaning supplies. Another study on investing in the stock market showed that, despite the fact that men traded stock 50 percent more often than women, women's portfolios tended to outperform men's.[1]

How does this relate to pornography? Porn works to fulfill men's needs based on instant gratification, yet the same quality in porn tends to deter women, who, in terms of sexual arousal, are looking for increased buildup and the ability to use imagination. Studies have shown that women, generally speaking, excel at long-term planning and also at what one scholar has called web thinking, the ability to integrate a variety of data.[2] Most pornography bypasses these types of thinking.

I believe these cognitive strengths of ours are also what make most young women fantasize about meeting Mr. Right, a man who is so in love with us that he does not even realize other women exist. As young women we plan our future weddings, name our future babies, and set up unrealistic expectations for our future Mr. Right. And then our long-term fantasy is destroyed when we discover that Mr. Right enjoys pornography.

Parental Influence: The Importance of Chastity

In addition to our natural programming, it is important for every woman to realize how she has been programmed by her parents and other authority figures since birth. Everything we were told by our parents about sex as impressionable young girls has impacted who we have become as women. Parents don't want to think of their kids having sex at any age, no matter if they are fifteen or fifty-five, but they *especially* don't want to think of their daughter having sex unless she is twenty-five, has a good career, and is married—or at least sleeping with a good guy who also has a decent career. Parents insist (and they instill these thoughts in their daughters) that a worthy mate is a man who is good to their daughter and who would also be a good father to their future grandchildren. Not that these hopes for a daughter are wrong; they aren't. I hope the same things for my girls, but I am also realistic, especially in how I communicate my hopes to my daughters.

It is my observation that most parents avoid telling their daughters the truth about sex. Many still imply that sex should be used only for reproduction and to meet necessary marital requirements, and that the chaste female uses her sexuality sparingly and conservatively. Instead, our daughters should be told that they might enjoy sex one day. They should be informed that sex is wonderful when experienced with the right person at the right time and with the right amount of knowledge and safety.

Generally speaking, American society, including parents, tells us from a young age that sex is dirty. We're advised that women are "sluts" if they have sex too early and too often, or if they have sex with multiple partners, or even if they happen to wear provocative clothing. Teenage girls and adult women call their peers derogatory names if they exhibit sexual behavior and shame them for their openness. This sexual shaming as an attempt to control the risks of sex isn't a new tactic. Many religions throughout history have implemented extremely restrictive sexual standards for population control, to reduce sexually transmitted diseases, and to control women.

The differences between how teenage boys are taught to think and act and how girls are conditioned is strikingly obvious. Girls are taught to be ashamed of themselves if they sleep with a guy on their first date; guys are taught to be proud of themselves, that the sexual "conquest" is a form of masculinity. Women who have multiple partners are "sluts"; guys who do so are "studs." Teenage boys nowadays are mostly told it is natural to masturbate; teenage girls are not instructed on self-pleasure at all or are told that it's dirty.

Eventually, teenage girls grow up to become sexually active adult women, many of whom are confused about their behaviors and their enjoyment of sex. The statistics about this are disturbing. Back in the 1980s, Ann Landers asked her female readers if they would be content cuddling in place of having intercourse with their partner. Out of the hundred thousand respondents, 72 percent answered yes, they would prefer a little cuddling and would pass on the sex.[3] That's probably because other studies show that only 29 percent of women routinely reach orgasm during sex compared to 75 percent of men. And finally, researchers from Massachusetts General Hospital in 2008 published a study in *Obstetrics & Gynecology* showing that 40 percent of women report sexual problems.[4]

It's very easy to see how we girls might transfer our confusion regarding sex and sexuality to pornography. I had to evaluate where my initial opinions of porn came from and what they were based on. After a few years in the adult industry, I began thinking about how severely unfair it was that men were so aware of their sexuality and the joys of orgasm while women were rarely, if ever, given this empowering information. I wondered why there was so much hatred and negative emotion directed toward sex-related products, which, when used in moderation, really do not have any victims. I ultimately recognized that I had been exposed to the anti-sex rhetoric at an implicit level since I never really received the "sex talk" directly from my parents. To counter that as an adult, I made an effort to expose myself to sex-positive attitudes and affirmations. I think shows like HBO's *Sex and the City* helped many women recognize that it was their right and privilege to enjoy sex with as few or as many partners as they wanted to, to enjoy masturbation, to feel empowered by their sexuality, and to embrace their role as modern and forward-thinking women, whether they got married or stayed single like Carrie and company. I find it refreshing that women have welcomed the opportunity to express themselves sexually.

I get it, though. As a parent, I know what I want for my daughters, and I sympathize with the fact that our parents did not want anything bad to happen to us girls. Instead of actually talking to us about both the joys and the risks of sex, it was easier just to make us feel dirty about it. My daughters are young, and I do not plan on having a sex conversation with them anytime soon, but when they are old enough I have sworn to myself that I will tell them the truth. I will tell them that an orgasm is great, but also that our brains require a lot of trust in our partner to achieve orgasm. I will tell them that it would be unfair to themselves to be sexually active without enjoying orgasm because they lack that level of trust with their partner. I'll cover the risks, too. I believe this level of honesty will encourage my daughters to grow up to make smart decisions and have safe and satisfying sex lives. Of course, this is all easy to say now, when I am years away from that conversation with my kids. Ask me again in ten years and see what my thoughts are then.

The Content of Pornography

The last major contributing factor to women's hatred of pornography is brought on by the porn industry itself. I don't mean the industry treats women poorly; this is far from the case, and I wouldn't be the first industry insider to say so. I mean it is the porn industry that produces content targeted to male tastes—*not* to women's. It's the same with mainstream Hollywood films. Studios put out big-budget action movies centered around exploding cars and a negligee-wearing Angelina Jolie shooting up terrorists. All of this appeals more to male moviegoers than to women. Still, we women go to the movies with our partners, hoping to lose ourselves in the romantic storyline featuring Brad Pitt, but if we were asked we would probably admit that we would prefer seeing the latest Zac Efron chick flick. Mainstream filmmakers purposely include emotional components in action movies to attract a larger audience. The porn industry, by contrast, doesn't.

Both action movies and pornographic films are fantastical, portraying unrealistic situations that for most women stir up negative emotions. A Hollywood blockbuster that features extreme car chases and outright violence usually leaves me wondering about all the innocent victims who are collateral damage. As a woman, this is what I am programmed to do: Consider the reality over the fantasy. Even when I watch porn for work, I find myself thinking, "Why would that girl get into a car with a stranger who has a camera? Doesn't she know the potential dangers of getting into a car with a stranger?"

I'll be the first to admit that porn storylines, for the most part, are laughable. For one thing, in a porn video there is never any chance of a guy being turned down, so that alone is unrealistic. And seeing all the sex action that's obviously geared toward the male character's enjoyment rather than the woman's is even more annoying. While screening a film I've thought, "Seriously, do you think doing it in that crazy yoga position with six-inch heels on would be comfortable? It hurts me just watching it!" For the most part, we girls do not want to see something that's way too big being put in places that are way too small. And then there are the sounds that the female stars make. The guy in the movie is saying, "You like that, huh?" while she keeps repeating, "Ooh, ooh, yeah, ooh, yeah!" There's no way she's enjoying every moment of sex enough to make her say, "Ooh!" that many times, right? The scripts are so bad that I've heard from many of my female friends that they don't mind watching porn as long as it's on mute. Yet men gloss over all of that as soon as their sexual brain is aroused. They couldn't care less if the situation is completely unrealistic, or if a full split might not be the most comfortable position for sex. In a way, when we women see porn, it's like trying on men's underwear and complaining that it doesn't fit right. Well, of course it doesn't! It wasn't meant to fit us ladies!

Adult entertainment, in general, is made for men. It is based on men's biological interest in getting right to the point. Male viewers want to have the general idea that the woman in the film is enjoying herself, but they aren't really concerned about how that happens. I remember an e-mail from one customer who requested that our lesbian scenes include less licking of the clitoris and use of sex toys. That guy is who porn is made for. Of course, I also think that he might be an extreme case, and I couldn't help but feel sorry for whoever his sexual partner is in real life. Seriously, no toys and no pussy licking? Really??!!

Although about 90 percent of porn productions are geared toward men, there are some companies that take couples into consideration, such as Wicked and New Sensations. Wicked and a few other companies, like Girlfriend Films, even produce material exclusively aimed at female consumers. Although some of this content might be targeting lesbians or bi-curious women, all of them tend to include plotlines containing romantic buildups and to feature women in their more natural form. Plus, they tend to have way hotter male performers than most porn made for men.

Let's not forget the erotic novels that are geared toward women. Their descriptions are just as detailed as any hardcore porn film, and women openly acknowledge enjoying them. *Fifty Shades of Grey* sold forty million copies worldwide to primarily female readers, most of whom can't wait for the movie to come out. I would imagine most men would be absolutely tortured by the idea of reading such a long book without pictures: "Why are there so many words before and after the sex scenes?"

Maybe with a little self-evaluation, a greater understanding of how our brains differ from our significant others', and an awareness that for the most part the porn industry isn't trying to turn us women on, we can take that *hatred* toward porn and turn it down a notch to something more like a *lack of interest.* We might even consider exploring the possibility of increasing our enjoyment of sex through the use of specially selected erotic materials.

What Do the Industry Critics Have to Say?

Hatred and confusion regarding sex and pornography are attitudes I'm very familiar with, having been exposed to them directly. I've even been targeted by this animosity. I've read articles and open letters from people who oppose pornography, and I've witnessed protests that have occurred at adult events. I've received letters and e-mails, addressed to me personally, that have wished me ill and have asked, "How do you manage to sleep at night?" (I've also received a lot of support from those close to me, as well as from a few strangers and casual acquaintances.)

I am not one who easily blows off a comment or chooses to live in ignorance, so I have had plenty of opportunity to evaluate what critics of the industry have to say. Typically, their complaints fall into one of three categories: feminist, religious, or social. There's enough history on each topic to fill a book, so I will limit this discussion to my opinions.

First, I consider myself a feminist. I believe all women should have access to the same opportunities as men and should be treated equally and fairly. I also recognize that men and women in general have different strengths and therefore are more likely to be placed in roles where those strengths can be utilized efficiently. The best example is found in professional sports. I believe that women should be afforded the opportunity to compete with men. If they are qualified, they should be placed on a team. I also recognize that it is extremely unlikely that this will result in 50 percent of athletes being female and 50 percent of athletes being male, since, in general, men have more muscle mass than women, making them more athletic. However, there are exceptions, and some extraordinary women could compete legitimately against male athletes. For instance, I have no doubt that the formidable Serena Williams could truly challenge and possibly beat any man she encountered on the tennis court. Even looking at golf as a sport, my own personal estimation is that if both men and women competed together, we'd see about 25 percent of the competitors being women because they are just as a capable of playing a good game as men. Yes, it's still a minority, but that's only because women's golf has not had as long of a history to draw larger populations of players.

The Feminist Viewpoint: "Porn Hurts Women"

Some feminists claim that pornography is demeaning to women. I just don't buy this view because pornography features both men and women. In fact, there is a huge market for gay pornography, which features only men, and yet this seems to be overlooked in arguments about exploitation of the actors or how the medium might degrade participants. Moreover, there are a fair number of pornography films featuring women in the dominating role, but most feminists only point out the instances in which women are submissive and sexualized.

I believe that sexuality is a characteristic that for many people, both men and women, is extremely strong. Many female performers in adult entertainment have very evident sexual traits, and judging a woman for utilizing this part of her makeup seems unfair. Typically, men exude more sexual potency, but if a woman chooses to exert her strong sexuality and take advantage of the opportunities available to her, it's only fair that she should have the chance do so without being judged for her decision. It would be like judging a female athlete because her physique or external appearance might suggest she is too "manly." Although such a woman may not represent the general population of women, feminism is about allowing a woman to utilize her particular strengths. Furthermore, women in porn make way more money than men do, and they have a somewhat easier job on camera.

It's odd to me that some feminists want to take away the power of our gender and its sexuality. We are women, and our sex does make us different. We can breastfeed and give birth to our children, and for the most part our bodies turn on our partners. Moreover, the art of the female form is appreciated by both men and women. This state of affairs is not demeaning to our sexuality. If anything, I'd say pornography is demeaning to men. It clearly identifies men's weakness and loss of control when they are exposed to something that turns them on. In a sexual situation, men typically are unable to think about anything else or snap out of their trancelike state as quickly as women can, mostly because women are sexually activated less intensely and quickly.

The Religious Viewpoint: "Porn Is Sinful"

Next, there's the religious point of view against porn, which claims that lust is a sin and the human body is sacred. I'm not a religious person, but I do recognize the overall intent and moral responsibility to do no harm to others and to treat others as you want to be treated yourself. Religious points of view around sexuality, in my personal opinion, are outdated for the most part. Through the ages, much of the religious instruction against having sex with multiple partners or before marriage was an attempt at population control, at reducing the spread of sexually transmitted diseases, and at controlling women. It was delivered during a time when birth control, condoms, and sexual education were not available. Our culture has evolved, but religion is usually the last to transform to meet changing viewpoints and step up to what is popular.

It usually happens after the fact, or sometimes never. It wasn't too long ago when religious groups heavily opposed sex before marriage, and nowadays that is rarely talked about as a topic except within a small number of very conservative denominations or sects.

The majority of world religions claim that the human body is sacred, and I, too, believe that to be the case. The human form is beautiful and capable. Healthy bodies are admirable, and sex is a wondrous part of who we are. The fact that humans want to watch a beautiful or even sacred moment does not seem unusual to me. After all, if churchgoers had the opportunity to witness a religious miracle, they would. Sex should be considered a biological miracle, and the fact that humans have discovered the ability to have sex for pleasure, and not only to serve reproductive means, allows us to be different from animals. I think this ability should be celebrated, not demonized.

Women throughout history have shared the miracle of childbirth with many others, including family, friends, and other women. With that thought in mind, I have always wondered why the moment of conception or another intimate act should be considered less miraculous. When men look at pornography, many are in awe. They are in awe of the human bodies portrayed onscreen and of the sensations they experience from the medium. After all, God gave us the ability to reach orgasm and provided us with brains and sexual organs that can become aroused and afford pleasure. I do not see why he would wish a lifetime of self-denial and suffering to prevent arousal when it does no harm to others. Of course, there are risks and consequences associated with engaging in sex with many partners or in cheating on your partner; those activities do involve other people, not just a video on a computer screen. Most people recognize the consequences associated with those actions.

What I don't get about some religious dogma is how much judgment is cast when discussing sex, sexuality, or pornography. Frankly, I always thought that judgment was supposed to be reserved for God himself and that unless you are directly harmed by another's actions, casting judgment only causes hurt. I would have more respect for religious institutions that seem to have endless hours and resources lobbying the government or railing against the adult entertainment industry if they instead practiced the brotherhood and fellowship they also preach. Maybe they could offer assistance to performers who need help instead of just casting them into hell for their supposed sins. Yes, there are performers who choose a career in porn because they have issues from their past. Most stem from lacking a fundamental amount of self-love, often a byproduct of having had to deal with an abusive relationship or other turmoil in their personal life. I believe religious organizations are better qualified to offer a helping hand to these people rather than simply judging them and hurting them through discriminatory behavior.

The Social-Welfare Viewpoint: "What About the Children?"

Lastly, some individuals and groups are concerned about the social impact of adult entertainment. I've looked into many studies on this subject, and there seem to be two schools of thought. First, there are studies involving sexually explicit material and its impact on the young mind. These studies show that sexually explicit images and even language can impact the mental development of a child or adolescent. It can morph expectations regarding sex and women's role in it and over-develop the parts of the brain that control sexual behavior.

I absolutely agree with this assessment.

I do not think pornography should be so readily available to young people. Children and teenagers should be kept busy in academics and other activities that develop their minds and bodies through healthy means. I'm sure there are some mature sixteen- or seventeen-year-olds, but overall, from what I've witnessed, they are not mature enough to completely distinguish fantasy from reality when they've been exposed to so little real-life experience around sex and relationships. As a side note, I'll even concede that some 18+ men who use typical pornography as a form of sex education and don't end up with a partner to openly communicate with, can end up very misled and confused.

Typical porn is not sex education. When it's used as sex education, men often misunderstand what their partner really wants during sex, enjoys about the act, what makes her orgasm, what a real female orgasm looks like (ummm yeah, for a lot of women, they don't scream "F___ me! F___ me!"), and how long it takes for a woman to reach orgasm. In real life, it takes a woman ten to twenty minutes to reach orgasm with foreplay and vaginal intercourse, while in porn videos a woman seems to orgasm every three minutes or as soon as a penis gets near to her vagina. So if you know a man who might be using porn for sex education, please inform him otherwise for the sake of all women. Or at least point him toward material that is created specifically for educational purposes, such as the instructional video *The Modern Kama Sutra* by the Alexander Institute.

The adult industry does a lot to self-regulate. In the past it did even more, but nowadays most adult websites are programmed with filtering software that can prevent access to a viewer when parental filters are present on the home computer. Adult sites also often have a warning label that is placed there voluntarily by the production house to prevent accidental viewing. Prior to the onset of the digital-age piracy issues, very little content was visible to a nonpaying customer, and the majority of paying customers were over eighteen because they needed access to a valid credit card. That's not to say there aren't some kids out there who would take their parent's credit card despite knowing better, but believe me when I say the adult entertainment industry does not want this to happen. Not only do we understand that we're producing content specifically meant for adults, but we also want to avoid perpetuating credit card abuse. The fewer fraudulent claims our accounting department has to handle, the better.

If there were clearer studies and corresponding laws regarding when the brain is ready to process sexually explicit imagery, I'd be happy to review the Pink Visual policy that asks users to be over age eighteen. For now, I figure that if an eighteen-year-old is considered mature enough to go to war and die for their country or cast their vote in a presidential election, they should be considered mature enough to view what they choose to view, sex-related or not.

Data also show that young, developing minds should not be exposed to violence. I am a supporter of these findings, and I find it interesting that there is much less public outcry over movie theaters packing their seats with fourteen-year-olds who can't wait for the next horror film or war movie to come out, and videogame makers competing over how realistic they can make their pretend violence (ahem, *Grand Theft Auto*, anyone?). Self-regulation seems nonexistent in these industries. In addition, I think parental education on the subject is lacking. As a parent myself, I think parents and guardians should be required to take one-hour courses every two years about the issues involving the children they are raising. Many parents are unaware of what the risks are when they give their child a cell phone besides the cost of the bill. They don't realize the phone may give their child Internet access and the ability to communicate with strangers or to send intimate pictures. Kids make a lot of mistakes, the majority unintentional, but it's part of being a kid. I'll never claim that adult products are good for kids, but I do believe that adults have the right to call the shots in their own lives and are competent enough to choose to watch adult productions should they so wish.

Now, there are two other societal concerns that often pop up when discussing porn. One is that porn demeans women and that by watching porn men subscribe to imagery that positions women as sexual or societal inferiors. This is not a supported assumption. On the other hand, the studies regarding college-age men who view pornography are quite interesting. As I mentioned before, the study completed by the University of Montreal showed that men who viewed pornography also tended to believe in women's equality. This makes sense to me. I have seen a lot of our fan letters, and I don't recall ever seeing one that spoke negatively about a woman. In fact, most letters either compliment the women in the videos or complain about the male performers. Common complaints about the guys are that they talk too much, are too "ugly" or "gross" to ever have a realistic chance with their gorgeous onscreen partners, or are excessively "corny" or "cheesy."

The second issue relating to societal concerns seems to stem from the fear that men who watch pornography are going to want to create their own "perfect" woman in real life. People who believe this do not realize that mature men have the ability to distinguish between fantasy and reality. Furthermore, this viewpoint also overlooks the fact that men are so in awe of being able to watch a beautiful, naked female body that they aren't even thinking about what they would change from a physical standpoint. Remember, that's how *women* are programmed to think; it's not how the aroused male brain works. If men thought that way, we'd be getting letters telling us how so-and-so porn star needs bigger boobs or has to lose some weight or get her stretch marks erased. The fact is, most men appreciate these flaws in women as part of their beauty, or they are so "in the zone" that they don't notice them when watching them onscreen.

So how do I manage to sleep at night considering the line of work I'm in? By researching and thinking through all of these issues. Also by writing this book. I realize that pornography can cause stress in a relationship, and I want to share how it doesn't have to. Making peace with porn is the right approach. Preventing your man from viewing pornography will only increase the amount of stress between you, and eventually it will backfire.

If we are to learn anything from history about this topic, it's that porn isn't going anywhere. Maybe we can evolve to the realization that sex and nakedness are natural. No, I don't think we'll all be living in nudist colonies (God, I hope not!), but I do think there's a chance that some of our prudish attitudes will disappear as more data about male and female sexuality become available.

5 | The Science of Sexual Arousal and Sexual Behavior

Another area where men and women do not have much in common is in the sphere of sexual arousal and behavior. Even without the degrees that would designate me a neuroscientist or a psychologist, I can tell you that the differences are pretty obvious. You've probably noticed, too.

Although a man might be accused of thinking with his "other head," I don't believe I've ever heard a women accused of thinking with her vagina. The fact is men are more quickly and intensely aroused than women, and whereas a woman can easily turn off her sexual arousal and return to a rational state of mind, I would never ask a man in a state of arousal to do any critical thinking or even, for that matter, to make a grocery list.

Sexual arousal in men and women involves both physiological and psychological processes, which result from stimulation of the amygdala, the part of the brain that controls sexual behavior. There's much more to be studied about the sexual brain, especially in women. What we do know is that *slight* differences between the sexes in the brain's reactions to various stimuli result in *vast* differences in behavior and in physiological and psychological reactions. It's obvious that men and women are physiologically different and are therefore aroused differently. Men get an erection and women don't, but there's more to it than that. When women are in a state of arousal, they experience vaginal wetness, erect nipples, engorgement of the external genital area (the vulva), enlargement of the vagina, and redness or flushing of the skin in the genital area. With continued arousal a woman's heart rate and blood pressure rise, and the skin all over her upper body may flush.

Arousal in men isn't nearly as complex; it all centers around the penis. Blood flow to the area increases, resulting in an erection and in swelling of the penile head, while the skin around the testicles tightens. Like women, men experience increased heart rate and blood pressure. During orgasm, both men and women experience strong contractions in the pelvic area. In women the contractions stem from the uterus, even if stimulation was focused on the clitoris. In men the contractions occur in the prostate gland and seminal vesicle, forcing semen into the urethra and out through the penis.

The psychology of sexual arousal is very complex, and much about it remains unknown. A large part of the sense of arousal for both men and women has a lot to do with their perceived gender roles; for women, there's often a need for intimacy. Hormonally, production of testosterone increases in both men and women during arousal; it makes sense that men already have a head start in the testosterone department compared to women.

Sensory Stimuli

Now let's get into what exactly are considered sexual stimuli for men and for women. For both sexes there are three main stimuli: vision, touch, and scent. To a lesser extent auditory stimulation can be considered a fourth. Visual stimulus is often the starting point for arousal in either sex. It can come in the form of viewing an appealing human being, either in person or through the media of erotic images or films, or it can involve the imagination, such as the visualization of fantasies when reading erotic novels.

Although the stages of stimulation can vary in their order, often the next stage is a desire for physical touch or contact, and for good reason. With a surface area of about fifteen square feet and nerve receptors over its entire surface, the skin can be considered humans' largest sex organ. Knowing this, it makes sense that touch plays a major role in sexual arousal. Sex educators and psychologists alike recommend lots of skin-to-skin contact for improving one's sex life and feelings of arousal. There's science behind this claim, with research showing that touch and physical contact can increase the bond experienced between a couple by producing the hormone oxytocin and can release endorphins that enhance feelings of intimacy. Massage, cuddling, tickling, and rubbing can all contribute to sexual arousal in both men and women.

Stimulating the body's so-called "pressure points" can enhance pleasure, too. The website AskMen.com put together a nice list for men to guide them in locating all the right pressure points in their female partner. It's a good read that I recommend you share with your guy when you eventually embark on a conversation about porn viewing and when asking him to address your needs, too.[1] Some of the names of the pressure points are self-explanatory, while others—not so much. They include: the Temples, Knee Kingdom, Heavenly Pillar, Rushing Door, Bigger Stream, Bubbling Spring, Wrist Rite, Shoulder G-Spot (that sounds good!), Gate of Origin, Sea of Vitality, and Sea of Tranquility. It's no wonder that some women report experiencing an orgasm without genital contact during massage! A good book for helping you and your partner explore each other's sexiest zones is *Touch Me There! A Hands-On Guide to Your Orgasmic Hot Spots,* by Yvonne Fulbright (Hunter House, 2007).

The names of men's pressure points aren't nearly as fun: the forehead, the neck, closed eyelids, inner thighs, lower abs, back of knees, ears, and feet. And speaking of massage, in many cases it is quite normal for a man to experience an erection while on the table. Reportedly, massage therapists are simply used to ignoring it. That's at least one benefit of being a woman. We don't have to worry about a large external sex organ hanging out there.

Don't Forget the Doughnuts!

Smell is another sense that can play a role in sexual stimulus. Some scientists say that when it comes to mating the sense of smell plays an even larger role than the sense of sight. These researchers look at humans simply as mammals and consider the conditions under which other mammals mate. Dogs are an obvious example of a mammal that directly employs the sense of smell in its mating ritual.

Humans do produce pheromones, essentially odorless chemicals that are secreted through the skin and seem to be somehow detectable by other humans. Some sources state that humans who secrete more pheromones have greater success with the opposite sex. Maybe single ladies on the market shouldn't shower just before they go out; why wash away the pheromones that have built up through the course of the day? Of course, a lot of sources cite this research as a way to sell "pheromone-based" perfumes and colognes, so take it with a grain of salt.

On the other hand, Dr. Alan Hirsch performed a study in 1995 on thirty-one men aged eighteen to sixty-four asking them to smell a wide variety of scents, including food, while researchers measured blood flow to the penis. These were the results:

- The pumpkin pie–lavender mixture increased male arousal—as measured by penile blood flow—an average of 40 percent.
- The black licorice–doughnut mixture increased male arousal an average of 32 percent.
- The pumpkin pie–doughnut combination increased male arousal an average of 20 percent.
- The smell of women's perfume increased male arousal an average of 3 percent.
- None of the scents tested on men actually diminished their arousal.[2]

So much for buying all those pretty-smelling perfumes! Too bad they don't sell doughnut-scented body wash. If we ever worried that our significant other had anything in common with Homer Simpson, here's the evidence.

Hirsch later conducted a similar study on thirty women, ranging in age from eighteen to forty, while measuring blood flow to the vagina (don't ask me how!). Unlike with men, certain scents diminished the women's arousal, including the scents of cherry, charcoal barbecue smoke, and men's cologne. Here are the top performers for increasing sexual arousal in women:

- The Good & Plenty candy–cucumber combination increased female arousal an average of 13 percent, as did the scent of baby powder.
- The Good & Plenty–banana nut bread mixture increased female arousal an average of 12 percent.
- The pumpkin pie–lavender combination increased female arousal an average of 11 percent.
- The baby powder–chocolate combination increased female arousal an average of 4 percent.[3]

What surprising results! I guess we should all roll around in some pumpkin pie and Good & Plenty candy with our partners and see what happens in the bedroom.

Seriously, though, I think it's telling that the number-one scent increased sexual arousal in women by a mere 14 percent while the number-one scent for men increased arousal by 40 percent. Whether through touch, visual stimulus, or even scent, men just experience a stronger sexual reaction than women do. This is important to recognize. We women can't really relate to men in terms of sexual stimulation when their level of arousal is on average double or triple ours.

Rather than regarding this contrast as a cruel joke played on the sexes by Mother Nature, I prefer to view it as a good balance. It's safe to say that if women were as easily aroused as men, we humans would probably accomplish very little, have a lot more children, indulge in many more affairs, and contract a lot more STDs. Look at the fact that some animals come into heat only once a year. I assume that's based on a natural need for population control.

Where's Barry White when You Need Him?

Last on the list is auditory stimulus, which has not been studied in depth. Research that does exist shows that both men and women tend to become more aroused with the aid of music rather than just noise. However, in a very recent study backed by the music-sharing service Spotify, respondents said playing music in the background during a possible sexual situation was 40 percent more likely to turn them on than the touch or feel of their partner alone. Of course, Spotify didn't measure blood flow to the penis or vagina in this study, nor do I personally buy the idea that men can get erect simply from hearing a song, but it definitely shows that auditory stimuli might play a larger role in our sexual excitement than we know. The top three songs for increasing arousal, in order, were "Dirty Dancing," "Sexual Healing," and Ravel's "Bolero."[4]

So now we know that a lot of factors can play into stimulating sexual arousal, and that men's and women's bodies respond to that arousal very differently, with the most common trend being that men are more responsive to sensory stimuli than women.

Which leads me to the brain.

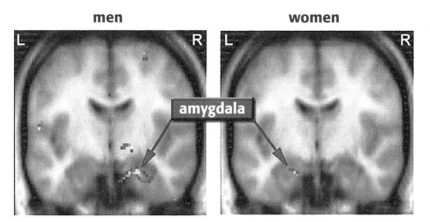

FIGURE 5.1 The areas of stimulation in the brain after men and women view erotic images

Your Brain on Erotica

Scientists studied the brains of men and women while they viewed erotic images to figure out what was actually going on. They determined that the amygdala, the portion of the brain responsible for memory and emotional response, also controls sexual behavior. Figure 5.1 illustrates their findings with images from the brains of typical male and female subjects during the experiment. In men, as you can see, not only is a larger area of amygdala stimulated; it's also more intensely stimulated.[5]

Seriously, girls, viewing this image must make us realize that we can't come close to relating to what our guy feels when he's aroused. I mean, we can consider what we feel and imagine multiplying it by a factor of three—or ten—but we can't really *relate*. I sort of assume that what a woman feels at the beginning of masturbation or foreplay is what men feel just from seeing some sexy pictures. Considered this way, it's much easier to understand why men enjoy pornography so much.

The same study, by Stephan Hamann and colleagues, revealed other interesting differences between the male and the female brain, significantly, that the size of the amygdala is larger in—guess who?—men.

Yes, men naturally have a larger portion of their brains dedicated to sexual behavior. It seems like all of our major gender differences stem from that fact. Additionally, the hypothalamus, which secretes hormones related to sexual arousal and also receives communications from the amygdala about sexual arousal, is larger in men than in women.

We can't win, can we, ladies? Well, maybe not in the area of sex drive. But despite having a smaller amygdala, women proved to be more proficient in the area of memory, including recalling emotional events more vividly. Although this means that, yes, what we remember from "that night" is probably more accurate than what our guy remembers, it also is one of the reasons why women are more susceptible to disorders like depression. (On the other hand, men are more susceptible to conditions like autism.)

Hamann has a convincing theory of why we women are much slower to react to sexual stimuli. Childbearing and child rearing are huge investments of a woman's time and resources, so evolution has provided us with the ability to actually slow down and think about whether we want to become the mother of a particular man's children. That makes sense when you consider much of history and before, but in the present age of readily available family-planning measures and condoms it creates conflict between the sexes. Maybe in another million years evolution will have brought women and men closer together in terms of speed and intensity of sexual arousal. One can surely hope!

Nature Neuroscience published an article in 2004 that combined research from Stephen Hamann, Rebecca Herman, Carla Nolan, and Kim Wallen.[6] This article provided even more interesting data about the research done on the male and female amygdala and its response to the stimulus of sexual imagery. One fact that stood out to me was that although men's brains were significantly more aroused, both the men and the women rated the sexual stimuli as equally attractive. To me, this means that we women like to think we know what's sexually attractive, but our response to that attractiveness doesn't compare to the strength of men's response. The other interesting fact was that both men and women rated sexual depictions of couples as more attractive and arousing than images showing only the opposite sex. The article further notes that the male is also stimulated in the hypothalamus region. In summary, "Notably, in no region did females show significantly greater activation than males at this statistical threshold."[7]

The amygdala is also associated with sexual orientation, and, interestingly, when it comes to emotional stimuli and memory, gay males have amygdala traits that are similar to women's. Although I have not run into any studies comparing sexual response in the amygdalae of straight men and gay men, I'd have to assume it is similarly intense, based on what I know about gay culture. You're probably not a gay man, and hopefully you aren't in a relationship with a gay man, but I thought this was an interesting point. Back to our topic....

Given the fact that as women we are pretty much at the other end of the spectrum when it comes to sexual arousal, one of the advantages we have over men in the area of sexual response is our ability to have multiple orgasms. A man's body is designed to prohibit ejaculation for a period of time after ejaculating. When it comes to porn viewing, that's probably a good thing. It means that when he's done with his "me time" he's actually done. It won't turn into an all-night event. By contrast, you could have a marathon of orgasms all night if you wanted to. You probably don't want to, but just sayin', at least you have that option as a woman.

Speaking of the Big O, whether it is with someone else or by yourself, achieving orgasm does offer a slew of benefits.

The Orgasm: A Bunch of Fun (Plus Some Health Benefits)

One major benefit of orgasm for men is increased endurance in bed. Women may joke about having challenges with how long a guy lasts in the sack, but for many men it's no joke. They are hardwired to come to a rapid climax, but they also want to know that they can please their partner. One way for men to do this is to practice on their own to build up their stamina through masturbation, without anyone judging them.

Another benefit of orgasm for both sexes is stress relief. Orgasm releases endorphins, the body's self-produced "feel good" chemicals. But here's the irony: Women usually aren't in the "mood" to come when they are stressed, while men seem to recognize the correlation between orgasm and stress relief and therefore want it even more during stress-ful situations. After the endorphins wear off, an orgasm also serves as a great sedative. Furthermore, studies have shown lower death rates, lower risk of heart attack, and lower blood pressure among both men and women who experienced orgasm often.

There's additional evidence for women about how orgasms help combat yeast infections, reduce premenstrual cramping, and ease back pain. Similar evidence among men is more controversial. One study from Australia showed that frequent ejaculation decreased men's risk for prostate cancer,[8] but many others were quick to judge the study as lacking enough evidence to make an actual statement of fact. I wonder if the study was right, and the question about its validity grew out of a fear that men would soon be masturbating everywhere and all the time. The fact is, from the Internet data I see, they are masturbating two to three times per week, whether their partners know it or not.

Of course there is also evidence that too much of a good thing can lead to sexual dysfunction. For men, excessive masturbation or mas-turbating using too much pressure can lead to a reduced ability to get off with a partner.

Bottom line: We women don't want to shame our partner over his "normal" masturbation habits. (If, on the other hand, excessive mastur-bation is creating sexual dysfunction, it's time to have a serious talk with your man and, if necessary, to consult a licensed sex therapist. These sorts of issues are touched on later in the book.) We want to avoid triggering or adding to sexual guilt that can contribute to problems like erectile dysfunction, which can affect his general happiness, mental stability, and overall well-being. Half of men report feeling guilty about masturbating,[9] and 30 percent of men report sexual dysfunctions.[10]

Given that this is a touchy subject for many couples, let's evaluate what is "normal." Most married couples acknowledge that the male has a significantly higher sex drive than the female and that sexual intimacy is important in creating a successful relationship.[11] Ninety-one percent of men in general report having sexual desire several times per week or more while only 52 percent of women report having sexual desire at that same level.[12] Don't feel too bad, though, married ladies, because according to a study by the Center for Sexual Health Promotion at Indiana University, married people are still getting it on with more regularity than their single friends. In the study, 61 percent of singles reported that they hadn't had sex within the past year, compared to 18 percent of married people, so your man should still appreciate being married, given the alternative.[13]

Still, it appears that most couples are having sex less often than the male partner would like to. Of course, there are many reasons why that's true, from biological and emotional needs to other issues, but strictly from a numbers perspective, it's not really fair for us women to not only deny intimacy with our partner but also to try to control our man's ability to take care of things himself. It seems like we should be okay with our guy masturbating, right?

I think so, but that leads me back to where we started this conversation: with a discussion of the differences between the male and female brains. We all joke about how men and women think differently, but for some reason we forget that's true when we are in the middle of a conflict with our guy, including disagreements about porn. I found an image that makes light of the differences, but the sometimes not-so-funny part is how true it is (see Figure 5.2 on the next page).

As we know, it's more than a superficial joke. Facts and studies highlight how different men and women are. Once the part of the male brain that controls sexual behavior is aroused, he goes into instant-gratification mode, but you're not willing to have sex right at that moment, so he decides to find a quick solution. And that solution is viewing porn and masturbating.

It all makes sense. Now can we accept it and resolve our other issues with porn? Probably not yet. Although we have a better understanding of how the male brain processes sexual stimuli as compared to the female brain, and we understand that there are benefits to orgasm, maybe we are still not yet being real with our guy. Maybe we continue to hold him up to a different set of values and expectations than we impose on

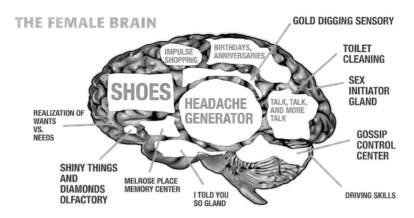

FOOTNOTE: The "Put Oil into the Car" and "Be Quiet During the Game" glands are active only when the "SHINY THINGS AND DIAMONDS" olfactory has been satisfied or when there is a shoe sale.

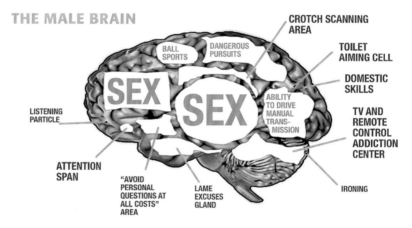

FOOTNOTE: The "Listening to Children Cry in the Middle of the Night" gland is not shown due to its small and undeveloped nature. Best viewed under a microscope

FIGURE 5.2 Internet meme on the differences between the male and female brain

ourselves. Deep down, maybe we still have this crazy idea that our guy has eyes only for us, and that all other women, whether in real life or in videos, don't do a thing for him.

Let's get real here, because by being honest with ourselves, we will be mentally healthier. The data is out there to prove that this fairy tale we hold in our minds is wrong.

Ask Yourself: What (or Who) Do *You* Fantasize About?

In a 2007 study on male and female fantasies that was published in the scientific journal *Hormones and Behavior,* women said they fantasized about something sexual once per *week*, while men claimed they fantasized about something sexual once per *day*. Interestingly, a 2012 study tracked the fantasizing of premenopausal women and found that they fantasized on average 0.77 times per day, and on average 1.3 times per day during ovulation. That's even more often than men claimed to fantasize in the earlier study! (The 2007 study didn't track fantasies on a daily basis but rather asked the subjects to look back over time and recall their fantasies, a less reliable method.) Women's fantasies during ovulation also increased in emotional content rather than in sexual content alone.[14]

A study conducted by the University of Vermont in 2001 showed that 80 percent of married women fantasized about men other than their husbands, while 98 percent of men fantasized about women other than their wives. That 98 percent statistic is even more evidence that all men enjoy porn of some sort, but the 80 percent statistic reveals a truth that probably most women would never admit publicly and certainly not to their spouses. Wait, it gets even better: Women in the study were way more likely to fantasize about other men *whom they knew personally,* while men fantasized about complete strangers or even faceless women.[15]

Now things are getting real! It would kill most women to find out that their guy was fantasizing about someone they know, when, in fact, women are more likely to be doing so on a regular basis than men are. Seems to me it's the pot calling the kettle black if we get pissed off to think about our guy looking at strangers in videos while we daydream about the hot personal trainer at the gym. Maybe our men should be more worried about our fantasies! Maybe we should put our issues with his porn-viewing habits into perspective. You've probably had fantasies about men you know, and you're not going to act on them. The chances that your guy is going to act on something from a porn video are even smaller.

Maybe the playing field is more level than we thought it was when it comes to sexual thoughts and fantasies. Especially considering how much more aroused men become than women, maybe we can acknowledge that healthy men manage to control their responses to sexual stimuli. Maybe we can cut them some slack.

6 | How Watching Porn Is Like Shoe Shopping

If you've gotten this far in the book, congratulations! The science behind the sexual brain is a lot to take in, so let's lighten things up a bit and enjoy the interesting topic of shoe shopping. Hopefully, you're beginning to realize that your guy is "normal" if he looks at porn, and you understand that there are things going on in his brain that automatically draw him to sexy images. But . . . it still irks you, right?

For one thing, it's not like he pulls up some porn online, figures out what he wants to watch, and in five minutes he's done, correct? No, he takes much longer, causing you to wonder why it's taking so long to…um…get the job done. Plus, if he's looking for sexy pictures, why doesn't he just use a photo of you and be done with it?

The answer to both of these questions has to do with shoe shopping. Yes, I said *shoe shopping*. Watching online porn is for men what shoe shopping is for women. Think about it. When you are at the mall looking for new shoes, you don't simply grab the first bargain-priced pair you see, deem yourself satisfied, and plunk down your credit card. Absolutely not! You take your time, wandering from Nordstrom to Saks to Neiman Marcus. You might even pop into the Manolo Blahnik store, to engage in a little bit of fantasy, some "shoe porn" à la Carrie Bradshaw, if you will. You try some beauties on, walk around a bit, admire the way your legs and butt look in the mirrors. You make it a point to enjoy the time you are spending on yourself. There's no husband, no kids, nothing else to do except enjoy the moment and find the perfect pair of shoes that you have been fantasizing about. Heck, even indulging in some online shoe shopping at Zappos.com can afford that same relaxing and fulfilling experience.

A Day at the Mall

So let's go shopping. Imagine yourself at the mall. Take in that fresh scent of new merchandise. You stroll to your favorite store, somewhere you have had success finding the perfect pair of shoes before, hoping you can score again.

Your man does something very similar when he is looking for porn online. Like you, he starts by visiting his favorite "store," the place where he has scored before. He might check out Vivid, or Digital Playground, or Pink Visual.

Now, back to you. You have a pretty good idea of what you are looking for: something sexy with a high heel and open toes, or maybe something you saw in *Vogue* the other day. Nevertheless, you have an open mind, and you just know that you will recognize The Shoe when you see it.

Similarly, your guy might have something very specific in mind. Maybe he's thinking he wants to see something that focuses on the woman's curves but is altogether real, as in no artificial parts. Maybe today a blonde might suit him, or a redhead. Maybe women wearing black leather, or a video produced in Europe. His tastes might vary, but he knows he will recognize what he is looking for when he sees it. Just like you.

Back at Nordstrom, you spot something right away, a strappy platform sandal embellished with glitter. You decide to give it a try. Looking at yourself in the mirror, you realize that although you like the fit and the shoe meets your needs, you think it might be way too early to settle on a selection. After all, you have time to kill, so you might as well enjoy yourself, right? You ask the store clerk to hold this pair for you.

At home, your man lands on the Burning Angel website and sees a video he thinks fits the bill, but it's too early to decide. It could be exactly what he wants; he just doesn't know yet without shopping around. So he tells Joanna Angel to hold that thought, just for a few minutes, while he opens a new Internet search window and keeps looking.

You are on a quest at this point. You go from store to store. You realize there is no rush—the babysitter has got the kids and the hubby is golfing. You feel good because you are knee deep in "me time," and it's all about you. Live it up!

It's important for you to realize that your guy feels the same way. You need time to yourself to take care of you. When he is looking for porn online the same thought is going through his head.

The shoes in the store windows catch your eye. It seems like the little darlings are truly *speaking* to you, calling your name, luring you in, making you feel sexy, elegant, beautiful, wonderful, seductive. Maybe you're feeling a sort of elation, a contact high, merely by engaging in the wonderful process of browsing through the merchandise. Of considering your options and waiting for that all-important connection with the one pair of shoes that will make your day.

Girls, as you engage in this type of shoe fantasy, know that everything on your partner's screen is doing the same for him. He is considering his options, he is engaging in fantasy, he is wondering how his choice will make him feel.

You try on various styles of open-toed heels, platform sandals, and glittery creations while imagining, "Where in the world would I wear these?" You place each pair on your mental back burner.

Likewise, your guy now has seven different Internet windows open, and he is still mulling over his choices.

Suddenly you come across a pair of fantastic shoes that you really love, but they aren't exactly what you had in mind. You needed an open-toed heel, but these are sexy red leather boots. You didn't think you were in the market for boots today, but they are pretty hot, and maybe you don't actually need the shoes you originally were shopping for. Because, frankly, you *really* want these boots. In fact, you don't know how you will go the rest of the day if you don't buy them *right now*. After much deliberation, you narrow your choices down to the top two. It's between the red boots and a fantastic pair of classic black strappy Manolos that fit all your needs and are exactly what you were looking for. Choices, choices, choices.

In your husband's parallel world, he runs into something he wasn't expecting. No way did he think a MILF clip would appeal to him. He had no idea that Lisa Ann in *Who's Nailin' Paylin?* would be his cup of tea, but, hmm, that librarian's bun and those dorky glasses and that little red business suit. There's something about it that just *might* work. At this point, he has replayed all the thirty-second preview videos, closing out the windows that didn't make the cut. Now he's down to his top two choices: Lisa Ann, in her sexy red business suit, or Lexi Belle, a hot little blonde who has been his go-to favorite in the past.

Happy Endings

You are lucky when it comes to shoe shopping. You can decide to go with one *or both* of your choices, which is exactly what you do. You say, "What the heck," plop your credit card down, and buy both delicious pairs. The transaction is completed within five minutes, comprising only a fraction of your whole shopping experience.

Your guy isn't as lucky. He has to choose just *one* of the videos because, technically speaking, it won't work for him to select both Lisa Ann and Lexi. And the next time he goes shopping he could be in the mood for something completely different, so it doesn't make sense to invest in both purchases. Once he decides, his "transaction" is completed in approximately seven minutes.

At the end of it all you're happy, and so is he. You had your "me time," you found some great merchandise, and so did he.

Internet statistics show that the average guy ends up watching only seven minutes of a porn video. The shopping process takes longer than the consummation of the deal. (As an interesting aside, I've heard that adult-video store clerks in the 1980s would tip off wives to rewind the tape by five minutes to see exactly what part of the porn flick "did it" for their guy. Since we live in an era of streaming video and the ability to delete browser history, we women no longer have that option if we want to gain insight into our guy's tastes. But I digress.…)

And to answer the question about why he can't just use a picture of you: It's not all about the porn, just like it's not all about the shoes for you. You already own plenty of shoes that are functional and do what they need to do, but it's important for you to have that time to yourself, to treat yourself. In other words, it's also about the shopping experience, not just the end result. Likewise, your man is looking for the opportunity to peruse the variety of appealing options that are out there. He, too, wants the whole experience, not just the end result. Remember, ladies, it has nothing to do with you, just as your shoe shopping has nothing to do with him—that is, unless you are both running up some big credit card bills. That would be a problem. Whether it's porn or shoes, no one should be breaking the bank.

Also bear in mind that when you shop for shoes you're usually looking for something new rather than buying the same pair over and over. Same with your guy. And that's a good thing. At Pink Visual, our Internet data indicate that most men bounce around among different porn stars and different genres. Rarely does a man become so obsessed with a single performer that he only watches scenes that include her. That doesn't mean he wants variety in his love life, merely in his fantasy life. Just as shoes would never replace your man (be honest, no one loves shoes that much, not even Carrie Bradshaw), the same can be said about porn stars and you.

Keep this analogy in mind: Porn stars are to him what shoes are to you. You don't want to always wear the same pair, and you have favorites, but you are not in a *relationship* with those shoes. You have much more of a relationship with your dog that likes to eat your shoes. Your man doesn't feel competitive with your shoes, and you shouldn't feel as if you are competing with the women onscreen. This theme is important for you to consider as we move on to the next chapter.

7 | Porn and Your Self-Esteem

We are well aware of how porn makes him feel, but let me address the elephant in the room, which is how porn makes you feel when he watches it. Girls, I know how it makes you feel because I've felt that way myself. Remember, I had those same worries. "Does he want me to look like that?" "Am I not good enough for him?" "Do I need bigger breasts?" "Does this mean he wants to leave me for someone who does look like that?" "Is our relationship ending?"

The first thing to realize is that he is not thinking any of those things when he's watching porn. He is completely *in the zone.* In fact, he's not thinking about you or your relationship status or pretty much anything else. He's not thinking about the fact that you asked him to get milk at the store that morning, he is not thinking about the deadline he has at work next week, he is not thinking about the fact that his buddy has asked him if he would be open to trading Tim Tebow for Eli Manning in their fantasy football league. His mind is a blank.

Remember, he's out shoe shopping! He's in a worry-free state of mind and is simply enjoying peering in the windows, so to speak, and considering his options. Frankly, it's only you who is thinking about your relationship and comparing yourself to some big-breasted sexual machine, because he is not.

Remind yourself of our analogy from the last chapter: Porn stars are like shoes. Men know they are incapable of interacting with them on anything but a superficial level. Even the idea that a man believes some deeper connection exists between him and the woman onscreen is absurd. If that were the case, men from all over the country would be flocking to Porn Valley (San Fernando Valley, California) to meet, woo, and marry their favorite porn stars. And that isn't happening. (Anyway, the majority of those women would probably shoot down a would-be suitor. Remember, they are doing a job. They are on the clock. They are working!)

Also, recall my photo shoot story. Remember how I asked guys if they actually wanted to participate in the live sex show with porn stars? The men who were faced with the opportunity did hesitate, think about the consequences, and even were intimidated as they recognized that no, they aren't male porn stars themselves.

Also remind yourself that female porn stars, those "sexual sirens," still put their garter belts on one leg at a time, just like you and me. We will talk about the mythical creature known as the porn star in a later chapter. For now, know that although they have interesting jobs, they go through the same stuff we do in their lives and relationships. They have the same issues, insecurities, and worries the rest of us have.

There's More to You than Just Your Vagina

The most important idea to absorb is one that I hope you know without my having to tell you. Your boyfriend, husband, or significant other is with you for more than just sex. There is more to you than just your vagina, ladies. Please say it with me:

"There is more to me than just my vagina!"

Think about it. If you and your partner live together, there must be a lot of areas where you mesh well if you can deal with each other twenty-four hours a day, seven days a week. Although men are more inclined than women to seek instant gratification, they are also completely capable of making good long-term decisions, especially when it comes to who they want to commit to being with, who they want to live with, who they love enough to marry, and who they want to have children with. They are attracted to so many other characteristics of a woman than just sex. It's usually our own poor self-esteem that makes the relationship all about sex.

We do it to ourselves!

It's in our head when we don't feel sexy, or when we're insecure about our abilities in bed. Our guy doesn't do that to us, we do.

I could probably talk myself blue in the face about this, but it's hard to build up a woman's confidence and self-esteem if she is already feeling low or worried about something like pornography, so let's consider the opposite scenario. Are you with your man just because of his good body and his big penis?

Of course not!

You might like that he makes you feel secure, that he's smart, that he's good with his money, that he's thoughtful and makes an effort to bring you flowers, that he knows you like no one else does, that you enjoy sharing moments together, that he's a great father and provider. All of those things are what you consider, not just that he can make you orgasm when you hit the sheets together.

The truth is, he feels similarly about you, and it's those thoughts that go through his mind first when he considers why he is with you. While he may also throw in, "And she's a dynamo in bed!" as an afterthought, he *is* capable of thinking about things besides sex. Yes, a healthy relationship does include a balanced and quality sex life, but that is not what comprises the whole relationship. Ultimately, it's a lack of confidence in us as women that can make our relationship all about sex or, on the flip side, the lack of it.

We're Sexy and We Know It

Now let's talk about our sexiness and how it compares to porn videos.

Simply put, it doesn't compare!

Hands down, the average guy would never turn down having sex with his partner—you—to watch porn instead. No matter how worried you feel about the hotness of whatever porn star he might enjoy watching, the real thing comes complete with emotion, more physical sensations of heat and moisture, mutual interaction, and a confidence boost for him. And whenever possible, he wants to make sure he's fulfilling your needs in bed, too.

When he gets to have sex with you and go to bed with you in his arms, he is thinking, "Yes, she wants me." He knows he will never get that from an adult video. He will always turn down his "me time" in exchange for "us time." In fact, even if you're not completely in the mood, even if you are just "taking one for the team" because you are tired and want to get to bed, he would still prefer any positive sexual interaction with you over a porn video.

If you don't believe me, I insist that you see for yourself. Once you realize that you beat out the thousands of porn stars in their professionally filmed and edited videos, I'm betting you and your man will both experience a boost in confidence (not to mention an increase in endorphins).

And here's a bonus: Not only is getting the real thing way better for most men than watching porn, getting half or even a quarter of the real thing is usually just as satisfying.

I gathered some tips from my guy friends on what would do it for them in place of a porn-watching session when their partner didn't want to go all out with sex. The first thing to remember is that there needs to be a two-way conversation in which you hear from him what turns him on about you and about having sex with you, and in which you share with him why you want to see him pleasured. Once he knows he has a variety of options to replace porn and still achieve release, he'll begin to ask for those options from you, or you can offer them up more often.

Here are some tried-and-true tips from individuals both inside and outside the industry. Your guy would love any of the following:

- your naked body in whatever position he prefers, with or without you touching yourself while he masturbates
- your positive words to reinforce how sexy you think he is, how big it is, how much you love his various parts, and how much you enjoy watching him climax
- your breasts, rear, stomach, or mouth as locations for him to finish on
- a blow job or hand job, of course
- you tickling his balls while he masturbates

Not all of these tips will work for every guy. Some men are embarrassed by the idea of being watched while masturbating. Just as you have insecurities, so does he. Maybe his are left over from being told at a young age that his hands would fall off if he engaged in masturbation. It can be a sensitive subject.

Once you have a healthy dialogue going about how you are willing to help him get off even if you're not in the mood for all-out sex—rather than the same old conversation about how much you hate his looking at porn or how porn makes you feel—you'll come to realize that he definitely doesn't want you to be a porn star. If you don't know how to have this conversation, don't worry, I'll get to that later in the book.

He's Not Being Unfaithful

Yes, he wants *you* to want to be sexy, and he wants you to treat him like *he's* sexy, but he doesn't want you to be a porn star. Studies have shown this reasoning is based on evolution. Women are more bothered by potential emotional infidelity, while men are more bothered by potential sexual infidelity. Evolutionarily speaking, men have a need to be sure about which children they've fathered, while women desire emotional fidelity to be sure the father helps raise the children.

Early man invested a lot of time and energy in establishing safety and providing for his family by hunting and building shelter. These were often life-threatening activities that he was willing to do only to protect those whom he knew to be his offspring. Although modern man lives in a much different world, with access to birth control and paternity tests, he's still wired mentally and instinctively not to want to raise another man's child as his own. Although supporting a family—even a blended family with stepchildren—may no longer be life threatening, it still requires a lot of effort and financial security, so I can understand why men remain programmed this way.

So what does this mean for you? Well, it means he doesn't want you being sexualized by other men, especially when he's not around. Yeah, he likes to be able to show you off from time to time when you walk into a room looking ravishing, but he doesn't want you to be dressed too sexy, with blow-job lips and disproportionately large breasts that trigger the attention of too many other men in a way that he has to worry about it. His worry comes in the form of jealousy. And the jealousy can be triggered when another man simply admires you from afar.

I'm not making a case for jealous, possessive men. There's a healthy level of jealousy and an unhealthy level, to be sure, but here's my point. I experienced this jealousy firsthand during the early years of my career. My husband realized that there were a lot of men in the adult industry and late-night parties with alcohol, and he'd get bothered that I'd shop for new clothes before every industry event. Despite the fact that I believed I kept my look professional and knew that he didn't have anything to worry about, he was still bothered. I invited him to an industry event in Phoenix, and, boy, was that a bad idea. My husband was very quickly annoyed by "a look" he saw another man give me, and the party pretty much ended for us right there. His instincts kicked in and he stated firmly that he didn't want his wife being sexualized by other men.

Of course, eventually he had to learn to compromise a bit and understand that both men and women enjoy receiving an occasional compliment or two from the opposite sex. Moreover, it's one thing to receive a compliment; it's another to take it to the next level, which is something I would never do.

When the tables are turned and a man sees another woman emitting that porn-star look, for the most part he's going to realize that he can enjoy looking, but she's not one to take home. You can take comfort in some of Ludacris' lyrics, "I want a lady in the street but a freak in the bed."

I say "for the most part" because there are obvious exceptions, especially in the case of some powerful men who believe they are above this rule (ahem, Tiger Woods, John Edwards, Bill Clinton, and countless other celebrities, sports stars, senators, and congressmen). For the purposes of this book, I assume your partner isn't a megalomaniac with an ego the size of Texas.

Overall, recognizing that your guy is not thinking about you or your relationship during his online porn watching will help your self-esteem. Take pride in all your attributes. Build your confidence knowing that your sexiness can beat out a porn star's any day. Take comfort in the fact that he doesn't want a sexed-up, hyper-provocative version of you at the kids' soccer game or anywhere else. He just wants *you*.

8 | The Life and Times of the Porn Star

So now I feel bad. I've compared porn stars to shoes and have basically said that most men don't want to marry them, but for the record and because I know several, porn stars aren't bad at all. In fact, they are really nice girls. You yourself are probably a fan of a "porn star" or two, or of celebrities who have slept with them, are married to them, date them, or are otherwise involved with them. (Can you say "Charlie Sheen"?)

When we finally understand that some famous people whom we otherwise like qualify as porn stars, it may help us realize how we are so quick to place negative judgments on sex or sexuality. I know, you're probably saying, "No, Allison. I do not appreciate nor am I a fan of any porn star."

Hmm, really? Have you watched *Keeping Up with the Kardashians* lately? Or have you logged on to TMZ online and checked out what Tila Tequila or Paris Hilton is up to? Were you ever a fan of *The Girls Next Door,* or have you watched Kendra Wilkinson in any of her reality shows? If so, then you are a fan of some would-be porn stars. Kim Kardashian, Paris Hilton, Kendra Wilkinson, Tila Tequila, Pamela Anderson, and country singer Mindy McCready have all made sex tapes. Heck, even Jimi Hendrix had a sex tape way back when.

"But hey," you may say, "those people aren't porn stars. They are victims. They had their private sex tapes leaked!"

That's what they would *like* you to think because that story sells sex tapes and gets them press on *TMZ* and *Entertainment Tonight.* What they don't want you to know is that they actually signed releases allowing their sex videos to be distributed, and that they are earning money from their sexy stunt caught on camera. In fact, they more than likely shopped their tape around to many of the adult entertainment production giants out there, because these very savvy women know that people like Vivid's Steve Hirsch, among others, understand how to sell sex.

Say what you will, it's the truth. It is pretty rare for a celebrity sex tape to be "leaked" into mass distribution because there is a very stringent federal law prohibiting such things. It's called 18 U.S.C 2257, and it is enforced by the FBI. If you want your image to be depicted on an explicit video, you have to show your ID, you have to sign a release allowing the tape to be distributed, and you have to make sure that all individuals who are portrayed in the tape do the same. Otherwise it's illegal, and there is absolutely no way anyone can profit from it. All adult studios—Pink Visual included—must be able to show proof of their performers' IDs should the Feds ever stop by and want us to produce our records. It's a highly regulated industry, which means there is no such thing as a sex tape being put into mass distribution by chance alone.

In fact, participants in the sex tapes that were truly leaked have generally done a pretty good job of preventing the tapes from being mass distributed. Both Hulk Hogan's recent mishap and our innocent *Sex and the City* star Kristin Davis had some personal videos leaked. Both stars were able to effectively put a stop to this. In Hulk Hogan's sex tape leak, the famous wrestler immediately put his lawyers in action to get the videos taken down from the sites that were distributing it and warned others of the consequences. His attorneys later filed a $100 million lawsuit against Gawker Media for a host of legal violations including invasion of privacy, showing that there are severe consequences to being involved in leaking a celebrity sex tape when most celebrities have pretty deep pockets to hire the big guns to make sure the tape goes nowhere. So there have been just a few real leaks, and I definitely wouldn't call Kristin Davis a porn star either given the steps she must have taken to prevent her tape from seeing the light of day. However, there remains a huge contrast between these true leaks and those other tapes that end up in mass distribution. There's of course an additional warning that these leaks are rare when it comes to celebrities who have the money to ensure severe consequences are incurred for distribution, while most private citizens are not in such a position. Unfortunately, in this day and age, it means that a lot of material that was meant to be kept private, like nude photos on a phone, can be compromised and put into mass distribution on upload sites as opposed to sites run by major porn brands. Usually the culprit is the ex-boyfriend, so private citizens beware.

Persistent Prejudice

Back to the porn stars you never knew you were a fan of. The women I listed have each made significant money off of a sex video. In Kim Kardashian's case, critics and fans alike believe that is how she leaped to fame to begin with. So it's not clear-cut as to why we would dislike anyone who uses sex or sexuality in order to make a profit, right?

Even though these celebrities pretty much fit the definition of a porn star, I can tell you they are treated with a lot more respect than the performers you might find in San Fernando, aka Porn Valley—especially when you take into account normal industry conditions, like workdays, contracts, requirements of the actresses when on set, and the stipulations the women set for themselves. Let's just say they are not "doing it" all day every day. In fact, some of the big stars who are contracted with the major production houses might only appear in six or seven films a year, a limit set to keep them from getting burned out.

At the same time, everyone is very aware of the abundant sex lives of many famous musicians, actors, and athletes. What do you think happens between groupies and rock stars after the concert? Let me spell it out: a lot of S-E-X. Tiger Woods had something like fourteen ladies on the side, despite being married at the time to the beautiful Swedish model Elin Nordegren. I'm definitely not condoning his behavior. I'm entirely against cheating, and I realize that the more partners one has, the greater the risk for disease (both catching it and spreading it). My point is that these stars are often idolized and treated well in society *despite* the fact that they have as much sex as, and maybe even more than, most porn stars. The difference is that they keep it off camera. Therefore, I would argue that it can't be the alleged promiscuity of porn stars that makes society judge them; if that were the case, we would have to stop being fans of a lot of our celebrity idols.

So why does society discriminate against porn stars and treat them harshly? This is an important point to consider, because over the years I've witnessed the prejudice against porn stars and how they are forced to struggle in both their personal and professional lives, especially in their efforts to build careers after leaving the adult industry. Story after story exists of ex-porn stars who hold university degrees (even the occasional PhD) and yet are fired after years in a good job purely because information has been uncovered regarding their past association with porn.

Here is a list of a few porn stars who are both sexy *and* book smart:

T. J. Hart: A multiple AVN Award nominee who also has degrees from the University of Colorado in psychology, sociology, and art.

Shy Love: Not only has she appeared in over 250 adult films, she also holds master's degrees in accounting and taxation. She passed her CPA exam and became licensed by age twenty-five.

Nina Hartley: One of the most famous adult actresses of all time. Initially Ms. Hartley got into porn as a way to pay for nursing school, but then she realized that porn stars were both compensated better and treated better in the workplace than nurses. She still became a registered nurse, focusing on sex education, an area for which she has become known both inside and outside the industry.

Ron Jeremy: Widely known as "the Hedgehog," the affable actor has a master's in special education. He chose a career in porn because he found it more profitable.

A.J. Baily: This young woman realized that her multiple master's degrees from St. Andrews University, in Scotland, came with a hefty tuition bill. Instead of pursuing her intended career of museum studies and anthropology, she paid off her bills by engaging in a business that was a lot less dusty.

Annie Sprinkle: She already had advanced degrees when she got into adult entertainment but went back to school to get a PhD in order to become a better porn star. She is credited for making feminist erotica mainstream and is widely known as a sex-positive feminist who has worked for years to improve the industry. She has a bachelor of fine arts in photography, a doctorate in human sexuality, and a few other university diplomas.[1]

Some adult-industry performers have been essentially "outed" after putting their degrees to use, most notably in the public school system. These are teachers who were fired despite having received positive reviews and having no issues within the school. Some taught younger grades, in which the students wouldn't be remotely aware of the teacher's past, and some taught older grades, in which a student might have caught wind about "something" from the teacher's past. These educators were basically fired for their decision to have sex on camera before they even became teachers. A quick list of fired ex-porn star teachers includes (by their porn star names): Tiffany Six (twenty-two videos), Rikki Anderson (fourteen videos), Heidi Kaeslin, Collin O'Neal, and Carlie Christine (*Playboy*).

Tiffany Six, also known as Stacie Halas, worked as a middle-school science teacher in California. Her past was uncovered when a student found an old video of her online, and she was fired for misrepresenting herself on the grounds that she had not listed her involvement in the adult entertainment industry on her resume. Critics of the decision to fire her argue that her past experience as an adult entertainer had nothing to do with her becoming a licensed teacher. After all, she'd rightfully earned a degree from an accredited university. Nor had she done anything illegal by working in adult entertainment, a legal industry. She just didn't want to highlight it on her resume. Furthermore, critics point out, the onus falls on the school district to screen job candidates by verifying the information included on their resumes. They should be performing employment background checks, which they did not do in this case. The consequences endured by Ms. Halas because of her past actions were, quite frankly, excessive, especially considering that she was teaching science, not sex education. Nor was she flaunting a "greatest moments" reel in class. As of April 2013 Halas was still fighting to get her job back by filing an appeal to the court's previous ruling that upheld the firing.[2]

Samantha Ardente was fired from a job as a school secretary, an occupation that involves little direct interaction with students. Crystal Gunns, a cafeteria worker, had appeared in about three adult movies and was let go once that fact was discovered by her employers. She appeared on *The Jenny Jones Show* in 2008, where she pointed out how harshly society judges a woman who has a past in porn. She said, "If this is about morality, our president-elect has admitted to doing coke, and he's our president. Does that make him a bad person? Bill Clinton smoked pot. Does that make him a bad person?"[3] Although it sounds like she thinks her porn star past was a poor choice, which I don't necessarily believe is true, she made some very good arguments.

Again, their past as adult entertainers was the only reason why these women were fired. At the same time, I've never encountered any evidence showing that ex-porn stars have abused any minors. This makes sense to me considering that their former career indicates that they enjoy sex with adults. It's a fact that most abusers are men who manipulate situations in order to be around vulnerable children in unsupervised settings. Often, these are mentally ill men who are unable to forge relationships with adult women. Yet somehow people have decided that female ex-porn stars shouldn't be around children—despite the fact that these women are entirely qualified for their current careers—to the extent that they would deprive them of their jobs.

In Britain, a school district was recently required to rehire teacher Benedict Garrett, aka Johnny Anglais, after suspending him in July 2011 for moonlighting as a gay porn actor. At his hearing, he compellingly argued that it was important for teachers to prepare students for the real world and that the real world included the viewing of pornography, which, he said, isn't going away anytime soon. He also stated that he believes that viewing sex is a legitimate form of entertainment. He said he has taught "young people to be open-minded, respectful, and tolerant of others for more than four years." In an appearance on *HuffPost Live,* Garrett pointed out that as a father he's far more concerned about teachers who smoke, are homophobic, or even are morbidly obese, all of which he said set bad examples for children.[4] He makes some interesting points, especially about smoking.

Then there's the story of ex-porn star Sasha Grey, who got booted from her volunteer position reading to first- and third-graders for the Read Across America program. Invited to participate because of her role on the mainstream HBO show *Entourage,* she wore a hardly provocative outfit of jeans and long-sleeve T-shirt, and of course didn't talk about porn, sex, or anything inappropriate. Still, she was taken off the volunteer list because parents complained to the PTA that she wasn't fit to be around their children (even though, of course, the youngsters had no idea who she was). I think any adult reading to any child for the purposes of education is a good thing, especially since so many kids don't get that type of parental involvement at home.

To further highlight the hypocrisy, Kim Kardashian recently visited a children's hospital, where she was received with open arms by kids, parents, and staff. There were probably plenty of children there who were old enough to do some Googling and see her porn video past. Does she get a pass simply because of the narrative she promotes insisting that her video was leaked? Is she a victim or a very smart marketer? I'm going with the latter.

Other performers have experienced discrimination in jobs completely unrelated to working with children. Kurt Wild was fired from Subway, Jessie Lunderby from her job as a corrections officer, and Mike Verdugo from his as a police officer. Even the husband of actress Jazella Moore lost his job as a town manager in Florida after it was learned that his wife had appeared in adult videos. In another case people complained about an ex-porn star's joining a volunteer rescue team as a qualified EMT. The woman wasn't even being paid for her work in the community!

Some individuals who work in the industry believe in the good they can do but have been discriminated against by American nonprofit organizations, so they've traveled abroad to volunteer anonymously for foreign nonprofits. At the same time, Tiger Woods—adulterer, diagnosed sex addict, and not necessarily a proponent of safe sex (several of the women he slept with reported his aversion to condoms)—continues to be invited to the world's most prestigious golf clubs and heralded for his achievements.

Beyond the discrimination endured by retired performers, many actors and actresses in the industry experience hardship in their personal lives due to their career choice. Some porn stars have been cut off from communication with family members. Even those who do not perform in front of the camera have to deal with the adult stigma. Joy King, a marketing and brand development executive for Wicked Pictures has publicly discussed the many obstacles she faced years ago as a single mother working in the adult industry. One of those obstacles was how to deal with the stigma, like when her thirteen-year-old son's best friend was told he would no longer be allowed over at his friend's house after the child's parents learned about Joy's career. Joy faced those types of obstacles head on, and in this case she handled it mom to mom and got the issue resolved. However, some adult-industry workers are not as good at dealing with conflict. Frequently, industry performers, camera crew, marketers—people in front of and behind the camera—respond by creating their own communities, their own "families," their own network of friends. They bond through friendly and romantic relationships, they double date, they get their kids together for play dates. It's an insulated, maybe even isolated, community because it is simply easier to be with people who accept you for you and do not ridicule you, discriminate against you, or make you feel miserable about your life choices. Some of the individuals I've gotten to know in the industry are far less judgmental and more open-minded about other people's choices than many on the outside. I think that is a testament to the humanity and the likeability of many of my colleagues.

Porn Star Onscreen—In Need of Match.com Off?

One of the most emotionally challenging and stressful situations for both male and female adult performers is, shockingly, dating. Yes, like the rest of us, many porn stars are seeking a partner who has the ability to meet their needs in a well-rounded way, not just sexually. Porn stars are multidimensional individuals, just like you and me, no matter what their day job is. They desire love, commitment, and the ability to connect with someone emotionally, spiritually, and physically.

Yet you can imagine the struggles they have in the dating world, let alone when they get close to another person and want him or her to accept what they do for a living: have sex with other people. Just as they would for anyone else, jealousy and other emotional issues crop up.

Even when two actors are dating or are married to each other, they can wrestle with jealousy if they perform with other partners. When this scenario occurs many performers retire, or opt only to work with their partner. Even Jenna Jameson, one of the most famous porn stars of all time, elected to finish her career with her then-husband. Although the marriage didn't last, it does refute the notion that Ms. Jameson was promiscuous throughout her career. It simply isn't true.

The True Makeup of a Porn Star

So you've heard how rough it is to be a porn star, but I also want you to understand who these adult performers *really* are. Beyond being sexually confident, they are generally very open-minded and tolerant of people's individual differences, as I've mentioned. They have a genuine appreciation of the fact that they are able to bring joy to their fans.

From an outsider's perspective, when you first see a porn star all done up, you probably would expect her (or him) to be a diva. As is the case in any business or industry, there are definitely a few divas, but more often you'll find that the actors are really sweet to each other, to their coworkers, and to the people in charge. Moreover, they tend to be very happy to meet their fans, male and female both, even though they are, for all intents and purposes, total strangers. Considering some of the stuff female performers are kind enough to put up with from male fans, it seems to me that their "creep radar" is set way too low—or maybe it's just that I have an elevated "creep radar."

I've witnessed several porn stars engage in deep and genuine conversations with men who appeared to be hypnotized by the fact that they get to be around a woman who has "gotten it on" onscreen. With clothes or without (at industry events, the porn stars are often more covered up than many of the female fans and wannabes), these women are simply a lot more tolerant than I might be if I were put in the same situations. Whereas I might be unable to stop myself from walking away in disgust, the actresses somehow seem to see the positive in the fact that this short moment may be the best thing that has ever happened in the man's entire life. Or maybe

FIGURE 8.1 "Porn Queen" Jenna Jameson and me, at an industry event in Phoenix, circa 2004

they just understand that this guy is their bread and butter, so they stand up straight, put on a smile, and act nice.

Many porn stars are well spoken, do volunteer work, pay their taxes—in short, they are good citizens looking to enjoy a career in adult entertainment and a normal life when they are not on set. Many are also parents. Some are single moms and some are married, but like most women their number-one priority is raising their child well.

The performers Stormy Daniels and Jesse Jane are both beautiful women who have been incredibly successful onscreen. At home they are moms who go through the same stuff any mom does: playtime at Gymboree, organizing play dates, worrying about their child's health and welfare, DVRing *Sesame Street*. Moreover, they work for companies that support their choice to have children. As a contract actress for Wicked Pictures, Daniels was able to take time off without pressure from the production house to return before she wanted to. Daniels has praised the flexibility afforded to her by Wicked as she acclimated herself to motherhood. Today, she balances working, caring for her daughter, and maintaining a relationship with her boyfriend, who works as an editor for Wicked. She says that although she works four very long days per month (that wasn't a typo, Stormy Daniels works four days a month, not exactly a "burnout" schedule, huh?), she also travels to make club appearances and go to signings, yet she feels she has the flexibility and the income to raise her daughter well with her partner.[5] The point is that just because a woman works in the adult industry doesn't mean she can't be a good parent.

Despite the example embodied by women such as Stormy Daniels, female porn performers are often judged for how they raise their children—as if a woman who works in the adult entertainment industry is incapable of distinguishing between what is appropriate for an adult and for a child. I play three roles every day. I am a businesswoman, a wife, and a good mother. Just as I am a professional in my field, I am maternal enough to know that my kids require certain things to have a healthy, positive childhood—and the female performers I have been around are no different. There are good parents and bad parents

FIGURE 8.2 Bree Olson, ex–porn star and ex-girlfriend of Charlie Sheen, on the set of a Pink Visual shoot without all the porn-star "glam"

FIGURE 8.3 Bree Olson, done up like a star

everywhere, in every socioeconomic class and profession. You can be an overworked, wealthy lawyer and be a horrible parent, or you can work at McDonald's, barely make enough money to pay the bills, and still provide wonderful emotional stability to your child. It goes the same way with adult film stars.

FIGURE 8.3 Lexi Belle at different Pink Visual shoots, showing she can play both the sweet, everyday woman and the dark dominatrix

Just One of the Girls

Like the rest of us, adult performers are petrified of being caught on camera without makeup or with a zit on their nose. I've been around porn stars when they are off camera, wearing their everyday clothes and looking like the rest of the population, and I'd have to say that some of the moms in my town who I see picking up their kids from school and doing errands have everyday attire that looks more like a porn star's "on camera" wardrobe than many of the performers I regularly interact with.

But I don't live in L.A., so I don't hang out with porn stars on a daily basis. This illustrates my point about how normal they are, because when I do hang out with porn stars, once or twice a year, despite the fact that I'm not close friends with any of them, they have always treated me well. They tend to be very open and to share their stories with me. Many ask about my kids and want to hear about my life as well. Even though I've been in the adult industry for many years, there have been

FIGURE 8.4 Porn Star Veronica Rayne getting makeup and styling with curlers before a scene, and Veronica posing after all the behind the scenes prep

times when I've felt intimidated by their stardom prior to meeting them, but have been immediately won over by their sweetness and free spirit (even when I've messed up and called a few by the wrong name).

Is it because most people don't have the opportunity to get to know a porn star that they feel it's okay to judge them about their choices, what they do for a living, or who they are as people? I think so. I also think mainstream celebrities, professional athletes, and rock stars are able to do a much better job of providing the illusion to the public that we can get to know them on a personal level. That's why they hire publicists. Of course, it doesn't help that our society struggles to become comfortable with sex. Years of negative programming about sex and sexuality (including things deemed "obscene" or "deviant") are engraved in our minds.

We can make an attempt to expand our ways of thinking to be more accepting. I encourage you to read the many stories published online about the lives of porn stars and who they are, what makes them tick, what drives them. Look for stories about Nina Hartley, Ron Jeremy, and Jenna Jameson—individuals who changed the scene and the market by taking action to thrust adult entertainment into the mainstream. These men and women are no slouches. You will find that their business savvy competes with that of many of the mavens of mainstream industry. Or read about a couple of my personal favorites, Lexi Belle and Alexis Texas, young women who are currently figuring out how to call the shots in their careers and to create brands around their names.

Maybe one day we can stop prejudging what porn stars *might* be like and instead give them a break, especially, for instance, when they are working to educate others or volunteering in their communities. If we really evaluate the validity of our fears, I think we can focus our efforts on more positive endeavors than judging someone—or getting them fired—over what is fundamentally a legal career choice made by a consenting adult.

9 | Mythbusting: What the Adult Industry Really Looks Like

Not only are many adult performers pretty good human beings, but the whole adult entertainment industry isn't what most people imagine it to be. It's actually kind of normal—or at least a lot more normal than what is portrayed in the movies and in the scandal-mongering reports written by industry critics. Let's just say that Boogie Nights is a movie, people!

The majority of beliefs held by industry outsiders about the companies and people who comprise the adult entertainment industry are completely false. Let it be said that I was one of those people who held some misguided notions, but the past twelve years of working in the industry have opened my eyes to the truth. And it's not scary at all!

Myth #1: The Porn Industry Is Filled with Dirty Old Men Who Wear Gold Chains, Have Hairy Chests, and Exploit Women

This statement is definitely not true, at least not anymore. Sure, it may have been that way before, and in the 1970s the industry did have some misogynistic undertones, but that has all changed for the better.

Let me take you back to 2001, when I started in adult entertainment. I was tasked with going to huge expo events held annually in Las Vegas and Florida. Although I was expecting to encounter guys named "Guido" who would leer at me while focusing attention on my chest and calling me "Baby," in reality I found an industry full of nerdy young men. Yes, *nerdy*. You have to remember that the landscape of adult entertainment has shifted; moreover, the industry has always been a breeding ground for technological development. Additionally, 2001 was the beginning of the Internet age. It was a time when technology was advancing at a rapid rate with the advent of digital cameras and web production. Young programmers, recent media-arts graduates, and wannabe Internet marketers like myself took over the industry. Yeah, there were some older faces and industry veterans around, and there still are, but they were more focused on hiring the best young techs they could find and giving these new producers a shot to see what they could do. And the environment continued to evolve as a lot of the young guys (and women) were able to implement their great ideas and ultimately climb the ladder. Not to toot my own horn, but I am a case in point of that progression, and much of it had to do with my tech background.

And there were women in the industry who were only there for the business angle, just like me. How could that be? Because the up-and coming guys were both nerdy *and* smart. They were smart to hire

■ **FIGURE 9.1** Our first adult tradeshow booth showcasing our "geeky" mascot

women who performed well. They saw strength in a woman's ability to stand out among all the men, hold their own, and establish successful business relationships. Not only were more businesswomen being hired by production companies—both in front of the camera and behind it—but some women even established their own successful adult businesses during this time. The men in the industry loved having these businesswomen around. They were nerdy guys trying to seem cool and to fit in, but they didn't want to be at an awkward cocktail party with a bunch of other guys (aka a sausage fest), nor did they know how to carry on a conversation with a porn star. Businesswomen were their saviors! They could talk business, make money, have fun, and still enjoy the "eye candy" that may have been strolling around.

Now, don't think companies just send token females to these events to mix it up. Adult businesses are pretty diverse, placing both men and women in a variety of roles. My company, Pink Visual, has about a sixty/forty split between men and women (the ratio reverses in leadership roles, forty/sixty. Furthermore, we have a roughly equal number of men and women doing jobs that directly involve looking at adult material, specifically, our video editors and graphics assistants. And my company is not an exception in this regard. The industry definitely isn't made up of a bunch of guys hanging out in the porno office. There are some roles in the adult industry that are still male dominated, specifically that of production director, but even that is changing as some well-known female porn producers make their mark. Consider the following women professionals who've made an impact on adult entertainment in front of the camera, behind it, and in other capacities. Some of these movers and shakers are among my favorite feminists and have greatly influenced me, both directly and indirectly:

Tristan Taormino: This young feminist is an author, columnist, sex educator, and adult film director. She's directed films based on her own sex education books as well as for Vivid Entertainment and Adam & Eve.

Belladonna: A popular XXX performer since 2000, Belladonna now runs her own production company, Belladonna Entertainment, for which she has produced hundreds of scenes.

Stormy Daniels: In 2004 this popular adult actress started directing films for adult entertainment company Wicked. She has directed thirty-eight adult films and has received three Night Entertainment awards for best director, among other honors.

Candida Royalle: One of the pioneers in couples-oriented pornography, Candida Royalle founded Femme Productions in 1984. As a director she has produced hundreds of films distributed by Adam & Eve.

Suze Randall: In the 1970s Suze Randall became the first female staff photographer for both *Playboy* and *Hustler*. She directed adult films from 1979 to 2005.

Jincey Lumpkin: Founder and "chief sexy officer" of JuicyPinkBox.com, a former lawyer, and a columnist for *The Huffington Post*.

Lux Alptraum: Writer, sex educator, and CEO of Fleshbot.com, which features blogs about sexuality and adult entertainment.

Violet Blue: Also a writer and sex educator, Violet Blue runs TinyNibbles .com and has written several books and magazine articles. She's often featured on mainstream television for her views and insight.

Joy King: One of the most well-known behind-the-scenes women in the adult entertainment industry, Joy King started as a marketing agent for Caballero Video. After being recruited to Wicked Pictures by company president Steve Orenstein, her public relations skills have been often attributed in positioning Jenna Jameson for mainstream crossover success and building the career of the "Queen of Porn." Today, Joy King works as VP for Special Projects at Wicked Pictures and has provided guidance as the company focuses on creating female-friendly adult productions.

Myth #2: The Porn Industry Takes Advantage of Women with Issues

Yes, it's true that there have been and still are many women who have "issues" of some sort and who end up performing in adult entertainment, but the industry does not take advantage of them. Being a performer isn't easy and it doesn't pay a lot. The system works the way most mainstream photography businesses operate: the model has to go through an agent in order to get booked for work. A talent agency will screen the potential models and performers to be sure they know what they are getting into and understand the pay rates. The screening also involves asking what the performer will and will *not* do and any performers she will not work with. This is very important. If a production house goes against the rules set by the model, she has the right to walk off the set. And many have done so. Moreover, the agency also works to ensure that the potential model is reliable and will fulfill her or his commitments. If a person displays obvious issues like intoxication or drug abuse, a reputable talent agency is hesitant to book her or him for work. Just like with mainstream entertainment, the agent will not get paid if the performer fails to show up on time or fulfill a contract.

On the production end of things, a studio head, producer, or director doesn't want to be put in the position where they feel they have to coerce or cajole a model into following through on the terms of their contract. As with any other business, pressuring a contract employee into doing something they feel uncomfortable with would be a huge liability to the company. Producers try to make first timers feel comfortable by inquiring after their needs. Sometimes the individual prefers to have only the camera operator and the photographer present on set. Many times, that can be accommodated.

There isn't much money in it for the performers. In web production, a female model gets paid between $700 and $1,500 for a thirty-minute scene that takes about six hours to shoot. The bigger stars' contracts might earn double that, but lots of performers leave the industry before making it to that pay scale. Ten to 20 percent of a performer's earnings go back to the modeling agency as a commission. Then they are responsible for paying taxes, as everything they make is reported to the IRS. Furthermore, they have a lot of out-of-pocket expenses stipulated by industry regulations, such as STI testing, which is done one or two times per month and costs over $100 per test. And their body is a commodity. They are the product, which involves costs for cosmetic "upkeep"—waxing, nails, enemas (yes, they always clear out their systems before anal scenes), hair, and so much more. It's definitely a job that's limited to women who really enjoy sex and who'd better be good at it, because if they aren't they are going to find themselves unemployed. "Dead fish" sex doesn't fly in the porn industry.

New and veteran performers must have a tremendous amount of sexual self-confidence. Most people would require a hell of a lot more money to put themselves out there in that way. I suspect that most women, deep down, have a "porn star" or "stripper" fantasy. They wonder what it would be like for men to worship and pay homage to the beauty of their bodies and to their sexual prowess. In reality, though, most of us wouldn't follow through on the fantasy because we fear that one potential critic. The porn star, by contrast, is sexually confident and secure and doesn't really care what a critic might say since she likes her body and what she is able to do with it. Adult performers also view sex as a performance, a performance they enjoy, but it's usually nothing like the sex they enjoy in their personal lives behind closed doors.

Many new models do leave the adult entertainment industry after a few months, but it's not because anyone took advantage of them or because they were exploited. Rather, their reason for leaving is usually related to the pressure put on them by family or friends, or because they realized the job wasn't the best decision for them financially or wasn't as easy as they thought it would be—there is actual work, time, and effort involved. It's about more than just looking pretty on camera while having sex. Trust me, there are a lot of women who can look good on camera while having sex; success in adult entertainment is based on branding, fan base, and professionalism. There are very few performers who actually make it big enough to be considered "porn stars" and who can demand higher pay or diversify with their own product lines. The women who do are the exception and not the norm. There hasn't been a star with a Jenna Jameson–level of fame since, well, since Jenna Jameson did it herself back in 2000.

In many ways the job is even tougher for men. Male performers are paid 30 to 40 percent less than women, despite the fact that men actually have to do *more* work and also to maintain an erection for hours at a time. Remember, a thirty-minute scene can take about six hours to film. It's much easier for a female performer to "act" her way through, but there's no way a guy can do the same. There are very few successful male performers in the adult industry, despite the fact that being a porn star is probably the dream job for most guys in their twenties. Pink Visual receives e-mails all the time from guys asking how they can become performers. Frankly, most never follow through when they realize that performance anxiety might burst their bubble. Here is another area where women have the power in the industry.

Few male performers have the ability to break into the industry without the help of a female performer. You see, contrary to popular belief, a woman performer is not "told" whom she has to have sex with on camera. Rather, she submits a list of her preferred partners during contract negotiations, along with her "no-go" list. If you are a male and are on a no-go list, good luck finding work. And if you aren't on a list at all, well, guys, good luck getting into the industry. The majority of successful men performers got their start because they were the male counterpart to an in-demand female performer. Once again, it's the girls who are in charge.

Bottom line: The end product in porn is sold to an audience of mostly males who happily pay the same price as they would for a Hollywood blockbuster—or more considering that some adult DVDs retail for upwards of $60. (Porn videos have dropped in value tremendously due to piracy and oversaturation.) So I always wonder why it isn't men complaining that they are being taken advantage of by the adult entertainment industry.

Oh, that's right, once they are in "the zone," they likely aren't thinking about much at all. That's a good thing, because I'm not sure what a porn boycott would do to America. Men everywhere would probably be close to bursting.

Myth #3: Porn Makes Men Accustomed to Body Types Women Can't Live Up To

The women in adult videos aren't runway models or Hollywood stars. Most new entries to the adult entertainment industry are of ordinary height and weight and evenly proportioned. Yes, the "classic" porn star may be overly busty, bleached blonde, and feature some amazing collagen injections in her lips, but new performers typically don't meet this description. They are more likely to look "normal." Really, even the classic porn star is more like a real woman than the excessively skinny and tall runway models who land on the pages of the Victoria's Secret catalog and whom most women compare themselves to.

Adult entertainment features a variety of body types and faces, all of which can be found in reality. The only difference is that women performers usually sport a lot less clothing, and what they do wear is a lot sexier than the clothes you would find at your local Target. I think if we were to analyze all the genres of porn, we might find that the body-type distribution is about the same as what is found in real life. A certain percentage could be classified as BBW (aka Big Beautiful Woman); others feature mature women, commonly known as MILFs (aka Mom I Would Like to…well, you know). There are films for guys who like younger women; there is even some grandma stuff (no joke!). There are big boobs, little boobs, there's hairy, shaved, pierced, tattooed, curried shrimp, shrimp scampi….Oh, wait, what was I saying?

Yes, a huge variety of porn features people who resemble what you'll find in the real world. It would make more sense to me if there were a myth (and there isn't) that men who watch porn expect to see nude or scantily clad women everywhere—just like it is in the porn flicks, when the plumber visits the housewife who happens to be lying around in lingerie. That doesn't happen (or at least not very often) because women dress for comfort and often dress for other women, not just to appeal to men all the time.

A related myth continually propagated by critics of adult entertainment is that porn encourages the objectification and degradation of women; that by fantasizing about the performer onscreen, a man will ultimately violate or humiliate the women in his life. Let me tell you that this couldn't be farther from the truth. The data we have collected in the form of surveys and open calls from our customers do not support these claims. In fact, many respondents complain if a film depicts aggressiveness toward women, or if it doesn't show the woman enjoying herself or with expressions of pleasure on her face.

This information might not have been collected through scientific means, but it is significant for a woman who might be struggling to understand pornography and the role it plays in her man's life. Men are turned on by the idea of a real woman having real sex, and it *does* matter to them that the woman is enjoying the experience.

Of course, I am talking about Pink Visual porn here. Viewpoints and attitudes vary across the niches found in the adult entertainment industry, and the opinions of a viewer who might be interested in bondage and other types of dominating behavior may differ from those of mainstream porn consumers. Still, the majority of Pink Visual customers are average porn viewers who generally don't get into specialty products. This isn't to say that the companies who produce those types of films are abusing or degrading women. It's important for you to understand that every woman who chooses to become a performer in any niche does exactly that: She *chooses* to work in a medium that might excite or stimulate her personally. Remember, ladies, you cannot degrade or victimize a person when they have the ability to say yes or no.

In closing, the idea of the "porn star" is just that, an idea. The female performer is playing a role and delivering on a fantasy. And your man knows this. Porn fans do consider the importance of the woman in the film, not just in the role of vixen, but also wanting to see her in a sex-positive atmosphere. As much as your man enjoys having a great experience with you, he doesn't wish anything different for the woman onscreen who provides temporary entertainment.

Myth #4: All Porn Stars Are "Broken Women"

Look, people are people, no matter what they do for a living. And all people have issues of some sort. There are adult performers who have issues, as well as adult performers who don't have issues. Just because a woman works within this industry doesn't automatically mean she has "daddy issues," was abused or sexually molested, or is a "broken woman." That's all a myth and frankly insulting to the perfectly normal women who find a home in the adult industry. There are plenty of stories of women *sans* issues who've chosen a career in porn. One of the most well known is Nina Hartley, who speaks openly about her career choice and about the adult industry in general.

Prior to entering the adult entertainment industry, Nina Hartley was raised by both of her parents in a loving and normal environment. She graduated magna cum laude from San Francisco State University with a degree in nursing. While in college she dabbled as a stripper. Her debut adult film, *Educating Nina,* was a huge hit. After college Nina continued performing in the adult industry because she enjoyed the work and the people she worked with. She won numerous awards for her performances and continues to perform today in mature-themed movies. She also produces her own line of instructional videos that piggyback off of her 2006 book, *Nina Hartley's Guide to Total Sex.* Nina is known for being well spoken and educated. She represents the industry honestly and positively.

There are many other porn stars whose stories of getting started in the business resemble Nina Hartley's. They come from normal, loving families, are well educated, and have had a variety of opportunities to choose from. Even the best-known male porn star in history, Ron Jeremy, is an example of this. He got his start in adult film because his girlfriend submitted pictures of him to *Playgirl,* but he also holds a bachelor's degree in education and a master's degree in special education. And you know what else? Ron Jeremy is a really nice guy. He once made my husband's day

FIGURE 9.2 Porn star, registered nurse, and sex educator Nina Hartley

by calling me on New Year's Eve just to wish me and my family a happy new year. I hadn't met him in person, but I had booked him for an upcoming "Live Sex Shoot." He just wanted to say hello. It's also been fun to be a fly on the wall when ordinary men run into Ron at industry events or trade shows. I've witnessed plenty of guys in attendance at the Consumer Electronic Show get all giddy at the sight of Ron Jeremy. They just plain love the guy. This thought also highlights some of my prior points regarding the differences between men and women. Many women would probably not have a giddy reaction to bumping into someone like Jenna Jameson, but instead feel threatened and put up their guard.

Yet, it's true, other adult performers grew up in or were exposed to abusive environments prior to entering the industry. There is plenty of psychological evidence showing that victims of past abuse sometimes engage in behaviors similar to what they were subjected to. For some it's a form of masochism or comfort; for others it provides the opportunity to release themselves from their past. Such tendencies can manifest negatively or positively for people who are drawn to working in the adult industry.

Without good psychological support, most survivors of abuse do not realize that some of their behaviors and choices are a subconscious reaction to their former abuse. They might turn to a life of crime, over-eating, or drug addiction, or enter into relationships that repeat the patterns from their unresolved past. They may wonder why they have these struggles. Most models who are new to the adult industry don't talk openly about their history of abuse or acknowledge that they might be stuck in a damaging cycle. In fact, many are still struggling to accept their past and hide their pain; they want to put their best face forward in order to be signed with an adult modeling agency. Usually, the truth comes out later, when the model may finally recognize that his or her choices over numerous years were consequences of abuse.

In any case, abuse victims in the adult industry ultimately fall into two categories: those who find that their work as adult performers has exacerbated the painful emotions around their history of abuse, and those who find that working in the industry has aided their recovery from the abuse by allowing them to be active agents who are in control of themselves during sex and are therefore no longer victims.

One story that comes to mind is that of Alana Evans, who entered the adult industry in 1997 at age twenty-one. As a survivor of an abusive relationship, and as a single mother, she sought to be able to provide for herself and her child. Alana always considered herself a person who was open-minded. She made a conscious decision to understand the distinction between sex and love. In May 2012 she appeared on *Dr. Drew*, where she said, "When it was time for me to get out of that relationship, porn saved my life. It gave me a way to be with my son—to be with him every day—[and] gave me money to take care of myself and take care of him."[1] Alana eventually opened her own business, PwnedByGirls, which combines two of her loves, sexiness and video gaming. As her son has grown—he's now a teenager—she's been honest with him about her past and has given him the tools to understand her career choice.

Every survivor of abuse has a different psychological makeup, and plenty of former adult performers regret their choice to enter the industry. I'm a huge supporter of increasing the mental-health services available in the United States, both to prevent abuse in the first place and to help those who have experienced abuse to recover. Personally, I wish the critics of the adult

FIGURE 9.3 Adult performer Alana Evans at the Pink Visual booth during the Adult Entertainment Expo

industry who complain that it takes advantage of people with issues would instead focus their energies on increasing support for mental-health care.

Myth #5: The Porn Industry Operates Like the Wild West

It's easy to see why people who are looking at the adult entertainment industry from the outside might believe this myth. It seems like a risqué, "living on the edge" sort of business filled with beautiful and scantily clad women who spend their days engaging in sex and debauchery. Many overlook—or are unaware of—the fact that adult entertainment companies have to do things by the book, like other businesses. At Pink Visual we have a human resources department, deal with accounts receivable and payable, handle payroll, and pay taxes. Really, how sexy is payroll? Not very. Furthermore, companies like mine must network with other adult companies, mainstream businesses, and banks. We have to be professional and know our business plans. This is important when negotiating with financial, technology, and other organizations; we have to show we are reputable so we can get a good deal on whatever it is we are going after.

Maybe you're wondering why, since we operate in the "shadowy" sphere of adult entertainment, we have to worry about everyday concerns like finance, contract negotiations, and the like. The answer is because adult companies work with distributors, mainstream cable and satellite TV companies, local communities, pay-per-view companies, and more. In Los Angeles and other places where production occurs, adult companies also work with the local governments to get shooting permits or meet the local requirements set forth by those communities that allow the production of adult content. Side note, besides California, New Hampshire is the only other state that expressly makes it legal to produce adult entertainment movies. The economic viability of several communities is affected by the industry. After all, adult entertainment creates jobs, and not just the ones in front of the camera. Think about the thousands of set operators, lighting professionals, editors, photographers, and sound technicians—not to mention the marketers, advertisers, office workers, salespeople, and countless other professionals who make the industry tick. These employees provide tax revenue that helps pay for public schools, local police and fire departments, and infrastructure like streetlights and road signs. Simply put, when you consider the impact adult companies have on the communities in which they operate, you can't say the industry doesn't matter. It does. My tax dollars and the tax dollars of my colleagues, onscreen and off, pay for the same things your tax dollars do. Money is money.

Moreover, unlike some other industries, the adult entertainment industry is highly regulated on many different levels. First, adult businesses like Pink Visual that operate in an online or virtual space are automatically classified as "high risk" by the credit card companies. That means a company like mine has to pay higher fees to be able to process credit cards, and we have to keep our consumer fraud levels lower than many mainstream online e-commerce sites. We are also regulated by a federal law called 18 U.S.C. 2257, which I mentioned earlier in the discussion about celebrity sex tapes. This law states that all adult-content producers are required to review the identification of all models who have their images depicted on film to ensure they are over age eighteen. Hands down this a good thing, but it does require that as a company we be meticulous in our compliance and recordkeeping, so that each record is saved in a database in such a way that it can be easily accessed and cross-referenced against all the performer's productions. We also maintain accounting records reflecting payments to 1099 (contract) workers. This is all monitored by the U.S. Department of Labor, the U.S. Department of Justice, and the FBI, as well as by local agencies such as CalOSHA (California Department of Occupational Safety and Health Administration). Complying with the requirements of these laws is taken seriously and is a huge deal for the industry. No legitimate adult company has any interest in working with a person under age eighteen. As an industry we have set up our own "policing" policies and procedures to prevent the exploitation of minors. Trust me when I say that no one in the business wants to have a minor on tape. In fact, several investigations in the early 2000s demonstrated that the adult entertainment industry respected this law.

The adult industry also regulates itself by having in place a system for regular STD testing among performers. This effort has been extremely successful in keeping the transmission of STDs to a rate that is even lower than the rate within the general population. Performers are required to be tested one to two times per month and in order to perform must share their results with their partners, their producers, and the organizations they are contracted by.

Despite our industry's success in complying with the laws and in self-regulating, another potential threat lurks in the backs of our minds: the possibility of being charged with obscenity. Although first-amendment fighters like Larry Flynt and many others have worked to secure a solid base for adult entertainment companies to legally produce adult material, the fact remains that obscenity laws are based on subjective opinion, and there are no clear guidelines. This means that

FIGURE 9.4 Kimberly Kupps, circa 2000

adult companies always have to fear being targeted by some branch of the government or even local authorities. When that occurs the business or individual who's been charged has to spend money to defend themselves, even if the government ultimately loses or cannot prove its case.

One good example of this is the case of Kimberly Kupps. Kupps lived in Polk County, Florida, where she produced homemade porn videos with her husband. She sold the videos on her website and also did webcam performances. Kupps' videos, which featured her engaging in sex with other women and men, fall within the same genre of professionally produced content that exists today. In fact, her videos were picked up by DishNetwork and other TV operators, all of whom have legal teams that extensively review videos prior to distribution and airing.

Although Kupps produced the videos in her own home and didn't sell them from her house, in 2011 she was arrested at home by the Polk County sheriff's department and sent to jail. Given a $7,500 bond and charged with fourteen counts of obscenity-related charges, Kupps knew that defending the case was going to cost her more money than she earned from her videos, which, at the time, were her main source of income. Kimberly Kupps was being held to the antiquated law related to community standards that I discussed earlier in the book.

Kupps and her husband attempted to fight the charges but finally agreed to a deal wherein they pleaded "no contest" in exchange for a single misdemeanor charge and a fine of $325. The remaining misdemeanor and felony charges were dropped, and Kupps and her husband eventually moved out of state. Her attorney, Larry Walters, said, "While I believe that these charges were unwarranted and ill-conceived, I respect Theresa's decision to resolve the case in this manner and move on with her life. The entire prosecution was a waste of tax dollars and will have no impact on the availability of erotic materials on the Internet."[2]

Because it is so easy to stir up negative emotions toward porn, performers and companies alike know that at any moment they could be subjected to a witch hunt by a local, state, or federal agency—pursuits that in my opinion waste taxpayer's money and needlessly tie up the limited resources of law enforcement and prosecutors.

10 | Finding Tolerance

So now that we've talked about your man's brain, the history of pornography, your self-esteem, and the workings of the adult entertainment industry, I hope you are able to take a step back and more objectively evaluate your feelings regarding pornography and your guy's relationship to it. While I certainly understand that every case is different and no two people are alike in their habits, desires, and turn-ons, the point of the previous chapters was to outline the norms. Maybe the information I laid out can help you come to an agreement with your man.

My aim is to help you find a compromise that works for both you and him in making pornography one less issue that puts stress on your relationship and causes you sleepless nights. American marriages are already under enough strain. The United States tops the list for the number of divorced people per capita, which leads me to believe that there are bigger things to worry about in a romantic relationship than what your husband or boyfriend is doing on the computer.

Dr. John Gottman, a renowned couple's psychologist, states there are two main reasons why couples divorce. The first is due to high levels of conflict, and the second to a loss of intimacy and personal or romantic connection.[1] In my opinion, removing the viewing of adult entertainment as a source of conflict by creating a policy of tolerance is immediately beneficial. More important, though, I believe the process of finding tolerance regarding adult entertainment—or any other interest a partner has—can significantly improve a couple's intimacy and connection. I'm not saying that if you accept his porn viewing all your other problems will dissipate. Other issues may still be present, and perhaps you will have to seek help in dealing with them. But getting over porn, so to speak, will provide you an opportunity to initiate a new type of dialogue with your partner—about a topic that previously may have triggered only stilted, uncomfortable, or even angry conversations.

How to Deal

Let's pretend (okay, probably not pretending here) that your guy would love to have sex with you five times a week. If we are being honest, that most likely doesn't happen. Maybe you're not always in the mood, or you're tired, or life just gets in the way of connecting intimately so often. I've been there, I absolutely get it. Furthermore, a lot goes into creating a quality relationship, and if your emotional needs aren't being met you probably don't feel like faking it. Whatever the combination of reasons, let's just say you don't crave sex as often as your partner does. Fair enough. If, however, you also insist that he refrain from pleasuring himself in the company of his hand and with the aid of some visual stimulation, I can tell you that you won't be any less tired and your emotional needs will remain unaddressed—*and* both of you will feel resentful and unfulfilled.

Both of you will end up feeling pissed off if you try to control his "me time." It's important that you realize this. Consider how you would feel if he decided to monitor or control your shoe-shopping time, the time you spend at yoga class or the gym, or when you decide to engage in your scrapbooking hobby or call your sister or best friend or whatever. You and I both know that if you aren't allowed to do what you enjoy and what entertains you, it's a complete downer. You know what you like, and if your man decided to butt his nose into your good time or control your experience, your day of trying on boots or attending a yoga retreat would be much less fun. More than likely you would rebel to try to get your way.

Well, so will he. He'll still find a way to do what he wants to do even if you try to control him. You have to realize that the time he spends viewing adult entertainment is the next best alternative to having sex with you, and he sees nothing wrong with it. Again, when he's doing it, he's in the zone and not thinking about you or your relationship at all.

Evaluate the Data

As a businesswoman, I'm trained to evaluate the data. So let's do so. Ask yourself how often he looks at porn. Based on our website statistics, an average guy in a relationship views porn roughly two to four times per week, with each session lasting approximately forty-five minutes. The numbers I see at Pink Visual are not unique; they are backed up by third-party reports. If your guy's "me time" is comparable to those statistics, recognize that he is completely normal in his habits. So you can stop worrying about that question and move on to the next one.

Now, if you feel that the time he spends viewing adult entertainment extends outside of the norm, then let's analyze that fact. Does your guy's porn watching interrupt the time you spend as a family? Or does he tend to do it when everyone is sleeping, when you're otherwise occupied, or when you aren't home? If you say that he interrupts family time with his extracurricular activity, then maybe you should consider talking to him about limiting the time he spends engaging in it to when you are not around. If the answer is no, he does not intrude upon the time he spends with you or the family, then appreciate the fact that he keeps his "me time" to himself.

Next, determine whether his porn watching is impacting your financial situation. If he's spending money like its water and running up your credit cards to balances that you can't afford, then that definitely needs to be addressed, especially considering how much free content is available on the Internet these days. While I am not a proponent of accessing pirated or stolen content, I am also not an advocate of going into debt over pornography.

If his porn expenses equal what you spend on activities that you consider personal time, such as drinks with girlfriends, shoe shopping, going to the movies, or anything else you enjoy, and your financial situation is such that you can afford this sort of fun, allow him to do what pleases him. On the flip side, if the two of you are in a financial pinch as a couple or a family, then maybe you both should make compromises and cutbacks.

Let's state the obvious: Many of your worries surrounding your guy's watching porn are based on a fear of the unknown. So a good thing to do is to let your guy know that you think you are okay with his watching porn, but you would like to know more about what he's watching, what he's into, and why he likes it.

I get it. This can be a hard conversation to have, but it's absolutely worth having. For one thing it can help you to approach the subject matter with an open mind. In fact, if the idea of knowing more about his inner thoughts on sex and what he finds arousing sort of turns you on, maybe you could tell him that. Certainly don't lie if that is not the case, but if you are curious and you believe it could help open up a dialogue with him, then say it. Then you must make a promise to yourself that you will not judge, even if what he tells you is something that might freak you out or that you don't want to hear. Again, I'm not encouraging you to step way outside of your comfort zone. But if, for example, he says that he really loves to watch two women having sex, remind yourself that this is not about you. This is about him and what he likes to envision.

Remember, fantasies are fantasies, and there are a lot of so-called strange or interesting ones out there. They might not be your fantasies, but people are often drawn to fantasies based on experiences that have affected them in ways they aren't even aware of. At the risk of repeating myself, I have to reinforce the point that *just because he fantasizes about something does not mean he wants to project it into his reality*. There's no need to worry about that.

A Conversation Can Benefit Your Relationship

By opening up this conversation you might learn something about your guy. For instance, a strong man might surprise you by stating that he enjoys videos in which women act as dominatrices, while a more docile man may enjoy more aggressive action. Most of the time these are fantasy situations that a man enjoys only watching in videos; he doesn't want to act on them. He might recognize that making his fantasy "real" just wouldn't be the same (often, the fact that it could never happen is what makes a fantasy so titillating), or the idea of experiencing it in reality might make him uncomfortable.

The best example of this is a gang bang.

Yes, a gang bang, in which, typically in porn, there are multiple males and just one female, who is the central point of the action. The majority of the time in real life, this scenario would not work. There are way too many naked men and penises in the room, which would make a straight guy feel really uncomfortable. Plus, the action requires a lot of men touching each other and having their penises in close range, which is *literally* a downer for most guys. Even on the set of an adult movie, a gang bang can be a logistical nightmare. No joke, ladies.

In a blog post on TBRDR.com, an author who goes by "Average Joe" followed up on an article titled "What Every Woman Should Know about Internet Porn."[2] He wrote about a struggle he had been experiencing with his beautiful blonde girlfriend, who *tolerated* his porn viewing but also got upset if he looked at certain *types* of porn. Essentially, the author's girlfriend had set out rules about what was okay for him to look at and what was banned or unacceptable. Latina porn was off limits, as were threesomes. She only approved of content featuring women who mirrored her "type," namely, blonde, beautiful, and Caucasian. The limits she wanted to impose didn't work for him. In his mind, she was controlling his fantasies, and he felt she didn't have the right to do that.

He writes, "She couldn't understand why I would look at these women if I found her more attractive. The reason is simple, it's a fantasy. With these women I can make scenarios in my head. They look like hookers and in real life I'd never go to a hooker. I'd be terrified of diseases, pimps, and jail. But in my little fantasy I can do anything. It's exciting to think of doing something I know I couldn't or wouldn't do in real life. I've also fantasized about beating the hell out of the guy who stole my car stereo but that doesn't mean I belong in jail for assault."

When I read this post I experienced an "aha" moment. I thought, "Wow, I've had fantasies and daydreams both sexual and nonsexual in nature, and I'd be pissed if someone tried to control those fantasies." I also realized that I completely trusted myself to be able to distinguish between fantasy and reality and that I should have that same confidence in my guy. Heck, the forty million readers of *Fifty Shades of Grey* probably aren't running around becoming sex slaves or losing their virginity to rich businessmen who want to tie them up and use a flogger on them, so they apparently understand the difference between fantasy and reality.

Average Joe said the same thing:

I understand where my girlfriend's insecurity is coming from but in truth it's unfounded. I'm happy with her and I am perfectly loyal. I think my girlfriend is one of the most beautiful women in the world and I'm not going to leave her for a red head, Latina, or midget. Men need to entertain a little fantasy every now and then and I think it's best for men to do this through porn rather than real life. Would you rather your man looked at porn of nameless women he'll never meet, or thought of the waitress at the place [where] he regularly goes to lunch? There's nothing wrong with an innocent fantasy, and chances are that nameless face on the screen will never leave her number at the bottom of a check.

You'll Both Be Happier If You Allow Each Other to Fantasize

As a knee-jerk reaction, you may want to influence what your guy uses to inspire his fantasies, but it won't work and it's not fair. If you find yourself having those thoughts, bite your tongue and instead remember all the fantasies you have that you don't act on. If you are an avid soap opera fan, think about how crazy those fictional, sex-crazed TV-based worlds are, and realize that just because you watch a show like *Days of Our Lives* doesn't mean you would ever steal a baby at birth, fake a pregnancy to the point of admitting yourself to the hospital with a synthetic baby bump, lock a romantic rival in your basement, or drug your brother-in-law to cause your sister to walk in on the two of you in bed. Outrageous, right? Just like a gang bang. It is *never* going to happen!

Instead, appreciate and enjoy how open he's being with you by having this discussion. It's good to let him share with you what type of entertainment he enjoys and what fantasies he indulges in, even if it is only by showing you a few pictures or telling you how he goes about discovering what interests him. You can also ask him what activities he might like to try with you in the bedroom (or elsewhere!). You don't need to make any promises, but putting it out there for consideration can enhance communication and intimacy between you.

Having encouraged you to stretch your limits a little bit, I also want to emphasize that it's entirely suitable, and even important, to discuss reasonable boundaries around your man's porn viewing. I'm not talking about trying to control the content of his fantasies, like Average Joe's girlfriend did. If you've asked him to show you some of the adult websites that interest him, you probably saw sites that displayed a lot of ads, maybe even ads for webcam chats. It's perfectly rational to set limits around the level of interaction he has with website producers, porn stars, and other women featured online. As discussed, as women we are very bothered by the threat of emotional infidelity, so you may feel ill at ease by the idea that your partner is having or considering having an interactive conversation with an adult cam model, even if she is five thousand miles away. Although a lot of men do participate in live cam interaction with adult models (at a rate of around $6.99 per minute, I might add), statistics show that *most* men do not, so the "average guy" theory doesn't stand up in this case, and it's your right as his partner to draw the line somewhere. On the other hand, it may not bother you at all. In fact, adult-cam customers are often couples who request exactly what they want from one or more performers, but we'll get into that in the next chapter.

At this point you see that your guy is normal in his viewing habits, he's limiting his "me time" to after hours, he's shared with you what he watches, and you've drawn some boundaries around what is and is not acceptable to you. Now it's time to have the conversation I mentioned in the chapter on porn and your self-esteem. Let your man know that even when you're not in the mood for sex, you would be open to doing something else—an alternative, if you will. Tell him he should speak up when the mood hits him and when he wants to replace his porn viewing with some sexy options with you.

Taking an understanding and reasonable approach with your partner on this subject will allow you both to know each other better and will reduce stress between you. In addition, it might be a good idea for you to indulge in some "me time" with your favorite sex toy. It might help you find new appreciation for your alone time *and* his.

11 | Incorporating Porn into Your Sex Life

If you are still struggling with finding tolerance, feel free to postpone reading this chapter until you are ready. Incorporating adult entertainment into a couple's sex life is not for everyone. In fact, even though I work in the industry I will tell you that I don't do it. Partly this is because I would have to distinguish between porn used for personal or sexual enjoyment and the fact that I work with it every day of my life in a professional sphere.

However, a growing number of couples find that watching porn together is a great way to spice up their sex lives, with the women enjoying it as much as the men. Some women, even on their own, are making dates with porn thanks to the wireless age and the fact that many adult-content producers are realizing that women are a viable and somewhat untapped consumer base.

Taking the First Step: Pornography and You

My first suggestion for getting started is to be sure you are in the driver's seat as you acclimate yourself to the material. Yes, it should be you who picks out the movie. That way, you can avoid some of the knee-jerk reactions that might still lurk in the back of your mind about why he is choosing *that* particular movie and what it means. Trust me when I say there is plenty of selection available. In order to find a video, you can try a couple of methods. You can go to the local adult-video store, which might feel a bit awkward, or you can do what every red-blooded man does: Stay at home and use the power of the Web to browse.

Ladies, just so you know, there has been a big transition in adult stores. Nowadays many of them aspire to be pretty boutiques focused on women. Although the freeway off-ramp adult bookstore still exists, it's a dying breed. The adult store may offer other perks such as providing you the opportunity to pick up a new sex toy or outfit, but when you're looking for a video, starting online is the best way to find the most variety. It is also the easiest way to preview the film before making your decision.

Google can be your guide here, and I can tell you the search engine is completely nonjudgmental. Or you can let your guy pick his favorite website that aggregates videos from multiple companies. Most of these sites offer "couple-friendly" categories, or genres that tend to show slower action and deliver more buildup in the sexual tension department. Wicked Pictures and New Sensations both have products with romantic story lines dedicated to couples, and they actively promote these offerings to women just like you. Even my company, Pink Visual, has recently focused more on couple-friendly productions with our

FIGURE 11.1 Ramon Nomar pouring Alexis Texas a glass of wine in Pink Visual's *Alexis Is Cookin'*

series *It's Her Fantasy* and *Erotic Mind.* "Amateur" and "solo" porn categories can also be good starting points. "Solo" especially might work if you have a hard time finding an adult video that features an attractive man. (Yes, I must apologize on behalf of the entire adult industry for all the hairy or dorky-looking guys we've employed.)

You may even want to start your search by finding a male porn star who is appealing to you and see what films he has starred in. One of my favorites happens to be Ramon Nomar, who coincidentally is from Venezuela, where my non-porn-star husband is from (do you think I have a type?). I personally believe that Venezuela should be famous for its attractive men, not just its women.

If you find yourself turned off by a film's cheesy beginning or by the script, consider fast forwarding or watching the movie on mute. Even if it's on mute, your guy will be thrilled that he gets to share this experience with you. Remember, he doesn't need the sound, he's got you.

Playtime

Now that you have your pick and have previewed it, grab your guy and tell him a little bit about the video and why you like it. This will steam things up as he listens to you talking about something that is potentially arousing to him.

Next, you'll need to select your preferred viewing location. If you are a high-tech couple you might have options ranging from watching it online from your PC, laptop, or iPad, to using AirPlay and accessing it on Apple TV or an Internet-capable TV. Whenever possible, choose a platform that allows you to watch your video in a comfortable place without interruptions. For most couples this is the bedroom.

Hit play (and maybe mute, too), cuddle up, and enjoy. It's probably best if you don't try to "force" any action; rather, just let things flow naturally. I think you'll be surprised at how arousing a porn video can be, and that's for good reason. Have you ever heard people say that men like porn because they are more visual than women? Well, that's untrue. We've already addressed the fact that men like porn because a larger part of their brain is dedicated to sexual behavior, and that when they're aroused they seek instant gratification (and porn is pretty instant). But we haven't yet discussed the fact that women are just as visually stimulated as men. Recent studies that tracked men's and women's responses to erotic images have confirmed this.[1] The reality is that you will probably be aroused by the video you've chosen. It may take you a little longer to become aroused than it takes him (he was probably "up" before you even pressed play), but you'll get there. You will most likely find that watching porn as a couple is a nice way to mix things up in the bedroom. It may also give you some new ideas for sexy action.

As you become more comfortable, you may want to choose a video together or even let your man surprise you with his pick, but don't rush it. You have already made a lot of progress in making peace with porn, but you may not want him thinking he has a blank check when it comes to involving you. It would become pretty annoying if he started telling you multiple times a week that he has a new porn flick for you to watch together. Enjoy your time in the driver's seat for now, and make it clear to him that this is to be considered a special occasion rather than an everyday occurrence. He'll still think you are the best girlfriend or wife in the world, even if you watch porn together only a couple of times a year.

Couples-Focused Pornography

If you are interested in checking out adult entertainment that has been made specifically for women or couples, there are some very good resources out there for you. I have compiled a helpful list to make your search easier.

Wicked Pictures

One of the largest adult-focused studios in existence, this production house was founded by owner Steve Orenstein for the specific purpose of creating movies for women and couples. Its website, www.wicked.com, offers over three thousand high-definition videos and forty-eight thousand bonus videos (scenes produced by companies other than Wicked, but which the company promotes and sells on their website). Wicked specializes in a variety of movie genres, but many of its films are full-length features that have story lines and plots.

Digital Playground

This production house recently went through a change in ownership, but one of the former co-owners was Samantha Lewis, who prided herself on creating adult products specifically for women. Although Digital Playground's widely varied material caters mostly to men, the company also focuses on producing full-length feature films containing plot and story lines. One of their most famous films, which won a slew of awards a few years back for its special effects and cinematography, is the widely heralded *Pirates*. Visit www.digitalplayground.com.

New Sensations

New Sensations focuses mainly on producing porn for men, but in recent years has opened up an entire line, *The Romance Series,* dedicated to couples. Watching the trailers to the videos in this series, which have titles such as *Torn, With This Ring,* and *Dear Abby,* will give you an idea of the story lines and the quality of the productions. I've found myself wondering if they weren't Hollywood movie trailers. Check them out at www.theromanceseries.com.

Pink Visual

Of course I have to mention my own company. We don't specialize in couple's porn, but we have started catering more to this market. We even have a couples-oriented line, *Erotic Mind.* Unlike other companies, which tend to produce full-length feature films in the ninety-minute to two-hour range, we mostly produce videos that last around thirty minutes. We figure that not all couples are looking for the full ninety-minute story to get things heated up in the bedroom. Our productions are simple, usually featuring attractive couples and implied situations to set the tone. You can check out our offerings at www.eroticmind.com.

Couples Porn via BabesNetwork.com

Two particular domain names, www.couplesporn.org and www.pornfor couples.org, will lead you to a website called babesnetwork.com, but don't be afraid. Although the site also features other genres, such as lesbian pornography, it allows you to specifically target what you are looking for.

Movie Recommendations

Here is a list of the top adult movies that have been made with couples in mind. Check out these titles and see what interests you.

Cry Wolf: With a plot that will leave you guessing about what is going to happen next, this film offers a roller-coaster ride of betrayal, friendship, drama, and, of course, sex. Starring Monique Alexander and Marcos Leon, it has a great script, a wonderful supporting cast, and fantastic cinematography. And it proves that some porn actors can actually act.

Tristan Taormino's Chemistry 4: The Orgy Edition: Don't be scared off by the title, ladies, it's not as bad as it sounds. Yes, there are half a dozen porn stars on the loose in the film, but still it's widely popular among couples. If the title is worrisome to you, leave it for later. You can work your way up to it as you become more comfortable with pornography.

The Opening of Misty Beethoven: One of the classics of adult entertainment, and quite possibly one of the greatest, this film is an excellent way to introduce yourself to the medium. By today's standards it may seem somewhat tame, but the acting is realistic and the cinematography showcases famous locations from all over the world. The plot is a variation on the *Pygmalion* and *My Fair Lady* stories. The film is a testament to what porn was like when being sexy was the main focus.

Eternity: A costume drama meets love story showcasing Wicked girls Jessica Drake and Stormy Daniels, this film has a great script and wonderful costumes. Directed by adult entertainment veteran Brad Armstrong, the movie is a treat. Also starring Randy Spears, Keri Sable, and Eva Angelina.

Compulsion: This porn happens to be a comedy. Based on one man's search for fulfillment, the story centers around a mountain-lion-attack survivor's group. Yes, you read right, and it's as funny as it sounds. Starring Randy Spears and Carmen Hart.

Love for the First Time: Also starring Randy Spears and Carmen Hart, this comedy is a parody of the mainstream hit *The 40-Year-Old Virgin*. (You will find a lot of pornos that play off of major Hollywood films.)

Faithless: This film was hotly anticipated because it was the debut of Kelli McCarty, Miss USA 1991, into hardcore porn.

The Texas Vibrator Massacre: You have to give props to the adult entertainment industry for coming up with some great titles, right? This film is a fine substitute for any mainstream horror flick. I can guarantee that Freddie Krueger never wielded a weapon like some of the maniacs in this film brandish their vibrators. Curl up on the couch and get ready to be scared sexy.

Brad Armstrong's Flashpoint X: Anniversary Edition: One of venerable porn queen Jenna Jameson's most famous vehicles, this plot-heavy drama dispensed with the plumbers and pizza-delivery guys. With excellent special effects, a terrific script, and high action, this take on the mainstream film *Backdraft* set a new standard in the industry.

Pirates and Pirates II: Stagnetti's Revenge: Mentioned previously, these films feature comedy, adventure, special effects, and a very big budget, all of which make the series among the most highly awarded productions in porn history. As close to Hollywood quality as you can get, they feature a galaxy of big stars, including Jesse Jane, Sasha Grey, Katsuni, Janine Lindemulder, Evan Stone, Steven St. Croix, and many others. Both the story lines and the sex will keep you and your partner engaged.

Conquest: Years before *Pirates* came out Jenna Jameson introduced the pirate genre to the adult industry. Produced by the couples-friendly film house Wicked, the movie showcases great sets, costumes, and props.

Island Fever Series: These films are all action and no plot—perfect for the couple that wants less talk and more hot playtime. Shot in tropical locations that provide a beautiful backdrop to high-quality cinematography, they feature slow-motion close-ups.

Dinner Party 3: Cocktales: A film that focuses on what couples want. The plot is centered around a social event that goes awry when friends start talking about, and acting on, their secret fantasies.

Marie and Jack: A Hardcore Love Story: The chronicle of a real couple who reveal their most intimate desires and moments. They discuss their relationship frankly and then have the kind of sex that only a true-life couple can have.

Debbie Does Dallas: Yes, it's a real film and it happens to be considered a classic by many. This is a must-see for anyone who is getting acclimated to pornography as it shows some very real bodies. The plot chronicles the story of some business-minded cheerleaders who decide to raise money by engaging in the world's oldest profession.

Manhunters: Focusing on some really hot bounty hunters who are intent on having dangerous adventures, the movie manages to make the action look real while keeping the sexual tension high. The good script makes this an ideal choice for couples.

Eyes of Desire: Directed by female porn pioneer Candida Royalle, *Eyes of Desire* takes a softer style of pornography to the next level. It incorporates a voyeuristic plot line and some great talent.

Edge Play: Starring Veronica Hart, this one is a perennial favorite for couples. The plot, edged with sexual tension, features two high-powered businesswomen who happen upon a world of fantasy where desires are fulfilled.

How-To Resources

If you want to go beyond watching movies together, plenty of books and how-to videos, written and produced by porn stars and production companies, offer ways to add variety to your sex life. These range from tips on how he can please you better to ideas for role-play and techniques for enhancing the mood in the bedroom. I encourage you to check out the products available. An improved sex life is good for any couple. Two examples are described here.

Jessica Drake's Guide to Wicked Sex

Porn star Jessica Drake, a contract actress for Wicked Pictures, is also a licensed sex educator. In this award-winning DVD series, and on her website, she counsels individuals and couples on trying new positions and activities, and on implementing pornography, sex toys, and other forms of erotica into their sex lives.

The DVDs feature the following instructional topics: female masturbation, basic positions, fellatio, and anal sex. With a goal of making viewers feel comfortable, Ms. Drake takes a very level-headed and non-threatening approach to subjects that many women might feel nervous about. Speaking with real couples, she highlights ways in which you can pleasure yourself while also pleasing your man.

Tristan Taormino's Expert Guide *Series*

Consists of five DVDs, each of which focuses on one of the following topics: fellatio, anal sex, the G-spot, cunnilingus, and female orgasm. The perspectives of both giver and receiver are presented, with demonstrations showing how to implement sex toys and other accessories, and discussions of subjects like how to introduce new positions and interests while keeping all parties comfortable, confident, and happy. The videos feature both instruction and real couples doing it on camera.

I've Done Some Research So You Don't Have To

Here's a short guide to some categories within adult movies to help you begin figuring out what you like and perhaps expand upon it as your tastes develop.

Hot Men

Let's call a spade a spade, shall we? Just as your guy looks for a certain type, I'm sure you also know what kind of man you are attracted to.

However, when considering porn, this is one area where you can easily be spooked. To make it easier, here is a list of some hot men you might want to Google.

Jean Val Jean: 2007 AVN male foreign performer of the year

Tommy Gunn: 2007 AVN male performer of the year

Julian: 1999 XRCO Award Winner and former U.S. Marine

Kurt Lockwood: three-time AVN Award winner 2004–2007

Sean Michaels: three-time AVN Award winner 1996–2010

Scott Nails: a performer in over 700 films

Steven St. Croix: winner of eleven AVN Awards for lead roles

Also check out the work of **Anna Span,** the United Kingdom's first female adult director, who is known for casting hot men in her productions.

Natural Bodies

I understand that some of your hesitation about looking at porn may be based on anxiety that the actresses don't have a body like yours. It's true, there can be something worrisome about big silicone boobs and a perfectly flat belly. In fact, it is possible to find real, natural-looking women. Many adult producers and directors realize that women want to see people onscreen who look like them. Check out the following choices if you are looking for normal breasts and tummies or regular-sized penises.

- **Comstock Films** makes independent amateur films that feature actual couples.

- Porn stars **Belladonna, Chloe,** and **Cytherea** are well known for their natural bodies as well as their enthusiastic performances.

- Classic movies such as *Insatiable* and the aforementioned *The Opening of Misty Beethoven* were made long before the days of boob jobs, waxing, and plastic surgery.

Industry Lingo: A Glossary

Let's end the chapter by defining some terms that could prove useful as you begin to explore the online world of adult entertainment. Knowing the jargon is the best way to avoid unpleasant surprises when you're trying to decide on a DVD or a VOD (video on demand).

AC/DC: If you guessed that this is a band, you would only be half right. In the porn world it means bisexual.

ATM: Yes, you might get cash at one. However, in adult it means taking something that was previously in someone's bottom and putting it in the mouth. If "TM" stands for "to mouth," I am betting you are smart enough to figure out what "A" stands for.

autoerotic asphyxiation: To borrow the Wikipedia definition, "intentionally cutting off oxygen to the brain for sexual arousal." I know that sounds dramatic, but remember that many people are turned on by many different things.

BBW: Big beautiful women, also known as women who might be considered overweight.

buggery: Anal sex.

candaulism: Wikipedia again: "a sexual practice or fantasy in which a man exposes his woman, or pictures of her, to other people for their voyeuristic pleasure." This is prevalent in swinger films or movies involving threesomes.

DP: Double penetration occurring at the same time. Buyer beware.

DVDA: The "D's" stand for "double," and the "V" and "A" stand for the names of a woman's anatomy down south. Combine the result with some math. "Double" means times two, in both areas. Four guys, two holes. Might not be something for a beginner to watch. I'm telling you this so you can be prepared and avoid selecting the genre by accident.

femdom: Films that feature female dominance over either a male or female.

fluffer: The person on a pornographic set who arouses the actors on film and helps them prepare.

full nelson: Also the name of a wrestling hold, this is a sexual position in which the guy is on his back and the girl is on top of him, also on her back. The guy takes his arms and puts them under her arms and behind her neck. She holds her legs behind her head, and he pushes her head down toward the action, making her watch. Kind of nasty, and, again, may not be appropriate for beginning viewers. On the other hand, actress Belladonna calls this one of her favorite positions. Know that in case you buy one of her movies.

golden showers: This involves urinating on a partner.

gonzo: A filming style in which the camera is acknowledged by the actors and often used to make the viewer feel as if they are part of the scene. Belladonna is an active gonzo director.

hentai: A sexually explicit form of Japanese animation or cartoon.

jack-gagger: A scenario in which a husband has other men pay for sex with his wife.

merkin: A wig for the pubic area.

MILF: I mentioned this term before in relation to Lisa Ann and *Who's Nailin' Paylin?*, but you only have to look to the mainstream *American Pie* movies for its definition. It refers to a "mom I'd like to f&^k." In porn, it's a full genre.

money shot: The messy climax scene, otherwise known as the end of the movie.

pig roast: A position featuring three people: one behind the woman and one in front of her. That's all I'm going to say about that.

podophilia: A foot fetish.

power tools: Electric or battery-operated toys used in sex play. For the record, you don't buy them at Home Depot.

queening: A form of domination in which you sit on a person's face to receive oral or anal stimulation.

skiing: When a girl is between two guys and she is simultaneously pleasuring them with her hands.

veggie scene: An all-girl scene.

wall-to-wall: A series of unrelated sex scenes with no plot.

Phew! I'm out of breath. Consider yourself prepared to begin exploring what's out there. Also remember that what I've described in this chapter is only the tip of the iceberg. Porn offers a whole world to be discovered. Don't be intimidated, and if you see something you dislike don't think it represents the whole industry. Close your Internet browser and start over. Trust me, it's not all as scary as it may appear.

12 | The Ongoing Female Sexual Revolution

I've mentioned that porn in general is not necessarily made for women; however, a growing number of women do purchase and enjoy adult videos. Even if you don't have any interest in viewing pornography as a form of entertainment, I encourage you to read this chapter and learn about some of the data surrounding the modern sexual revolution. If you're a woman who is already intrigued by (or at least open to) the idea of viewing porn, you can consider yourself a part of the female sexual revolution. Congrats!

Yes, the sexual revolution that was kicked off a generation ago continues, with more and more women realizing that it's perfectly okay not only to enjoy sex but also to have their sexual appetites catered to by their partners (singular or plural). Despite the recession, the sex-toy industry has boomed over the past few years. A little investigation will reveal that there has been a transformation in how manufacturers and store owners aim to appeal to women. In a 2004 study, 40 percent of women said they used or had used sex toys; five years later the number had increased to over 53 percent.[1] In another ten years I believe it will easily top 75 percent. Shows like *Sex and the City* helped to bring these realities into the mainstream spotlight (remember the episode involving the now famous "Rabbit"?). Bottom line: many women want to enjoy orgasms even if they are not in a relationship. Or if they are, they want to be pleasured when their guy isn't around. Or they want to find ways to improve sex with their partner. The good news is that 70 percent of men say they are not intimidated if their female partner chooses to use a sex toy or vibrator.

What's wrong with a little extra enjoyment for the ladies? Nothing at all. As discussed, the female orgasm provides tons of physical benefits, for example, preventing and helping to remedy yeast infections and improving sleep patterns. A smaller portion of women who own sex toys also rely on porn when formulating a plan of action for their alone time. However, many women find that much of the porn available in adult stores and on the Internet bothers them. They dislike either the context, or the fact that it is clearly meant for a male audience. Even when you modify the online search term to "porn for women" it often leads to lesbian porn, which might not interest a straight woman.

So what is a girl to do?

Feeling Kinky: The E-Book Phenomenon

For the most part, women still turn to erotic novels for their "me time" or to assist them in getting in the mood. Remember all that web data I listed early in the book demonstrating the huge numbers of online searches for porn? Well, similar data are available for erotic and romantic novels. Overall, it's been a tough time for the publishing industry, with net revenues decreasing by $9.5 billion in 2011. Yet the genre of romance fiction actually increased in revenue in 2011, from $1.355 billion to $1.368 billion.[2] Even more interesting is the fact that although only about 26 percent of books within the entire book-publishing industry are purchased as e-books, e-book sales of romances doubled in one year, up from 22 percent in the first quarter of 2011 to 44 percent in the first quarter of 2012. When it comes to romance fiction, both overall revenues and e-book percentages are trending upward. (Remember our discussion earlier about the fact that readers of erotic fiction no longer have to make their steamy purchases in public, thanks to e-readers?) Also take a look at Figure 12.1, which shows trends in Google searches for "romance fiction" and "erotic novel." Both are growing, but I find it especially fascinating that in 2012 searches for "erotic novel" exceeded searches for "romance fiction."

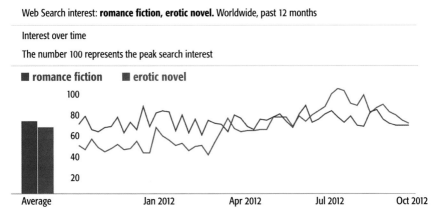

Web Search interest: **romance fiction, erotic novel.** Worldwide, past 12 months

Interest over time

The number 100 represents the peak search interest

FIGURE 12.1 Google Trends showing the growth of searches for "romance fiction" and "erotic novel"

We women aren't always honest with ourselves or others about the fact that we have erotic fantasies. No wonder, since most of us have been programmed to some extent to believe that sex is dirty. Nonetheless, the statistics show that more and more women seek sexual stimulation through books and other media. What about something that requires a lot less reading than a romance novel? Something in the field of visual stimulation? What about porn for women?

Women Porn Viewers: An Emerging Demographic

As discussed, a growing number of women want to see men and women in sex videos, but they aren't interested in the typical movies the porn industry puts out for men. Typically, women consumers, myself included, aren't interested in the male fantasy in which a plumber shows up and seduces the housewife, or the housekeeper happens to like polishing the piano naked. I know for a fact that I would never, ever say, "Glad you just fixed my shitter. How about now you strip down and make me howl?" (Who knows, though? Maybe you have a secret plumber fetish.)

Still, we women do get turned on. Maybe we fantasize about a really sexy guy like George Clooney, Matt Damon, or, hey, even Edward Cullen from *Twilight* sweeping us off our feet and ravaging us. (Keep in mind that *Fifty Shades of Grey* got its start as *Twilight* fan fiction.) Maybe we have a secret, lusty crush on a coworker, or on that guy who works at our favorite shoe store—a crush we know we'd never act on. I'll be the first to admit that sometimes a guy whom I never consciously thought of in a sexual way pops into a dream or two, and after that I don't mind putting him into my fantasies. That's how David Letterman became one of the names in my mental little black book. You just never know, do you?

Of course, Hollywood excels at creating sexual tension and emotional buildup. *The Black Swan* is one of the recent films that did this very well. The website Mr. Skin not only showcases nude celebrities but also keeps a log of sexy movies and TV episodes.

As mentioned, a few adult entertainment companies, such as Wicked and New Sensations, have begun focusing on creating porn for women because they understand that women viewers' needs and interests are different from those of men. Wicked even has a whole line of films that are produced *by* women *for* women, a move that can take some of the confused guilt out of the purchase process for the female consumer. Another line of products that appeals to both straight and lesbian women is the one produced by Jincey Lumpkin for Juicy Pink Box. Despite the fact that she produces lesbian erotica, she's received letters from many straight women thanking her for her productions that allow them to fantasize a bit about other women.

Besides producing and directing adult entertainment, Jincey Lumpkin is an attorney, a writer for *The Huffington Post*, and a sex-positive feminist. She and I are both supporters and critics of the adult entertainment industry, and we hope that our feedback will influence people in the business to act more responsibly and improve the industry's reputation. We also are both passionate about the idea of delivering products that meet the needs of women as they explore and enhance their sexuality. We hope one day to co-create a line of products ranging from videos to erotic books and articles to everyday products. Until Jincey and I, or someone else, find a way to serve this growing market, I encourage you, dear reader, to keep revolutionizing your sex life, in whatever ways work for you and reach out to support sex-positive women.

13 | A Recap: Five Lessons from My Career in Porn

Girls, it has been quite a ride. It's safe to say that when I went on that job interview with the porn company behind the 7-Eleven, I never imagined my journey would still be progressing a dozen years later. I also never imagined that I would meet so many great people in the field of adult entertainment, nor that I would become CEO of an adult studio. I've learned so much along the way.

It's interesting to think about how we all have the ability to alter our opinions, our beliefs, our outlook on life. We have unlimited chances to change our mind or consider other points of view. I know that if I had refused to open my mind—if I hadn't agreed to go on that first interview with TopBucks so many moons ago—I would have missed out on something great.

Likewise, ladies, I applaud you for being open-minded enough to pick up this book and read what I have to say. I know that engaging in a discussion about sex and relationships can be stressful, especially when we have society and politicians and religious leaders—jeez, even family members and parents—telling us who we should be as women, what we should enjoy, what beliefs we should subscribe to, and what our choices mean. Stepping outside of your comfort zone can be really hard, especially when you are also worried about the guy you love and about the impact of an outside influence like pornography on your relationship.

Like most people, there are things I regret from my past, and I certainly recognize that I am not perfect, but in light of everything, I do believe I am a better person all around because of my career in porn. My self-esteem has improved—in terms of my body image, my sexuality, and in other areas—and it's all due to the lessons I've shared with you in this book. I call them "The Five Lessons of Porn," and I've summarized them below.

Lesson #1: All Men Enjoy Porn

It's true, ladies, and there isn't any other way to say it. If your guy watches porn, he is *normal*. It is part of men's nature and has been since prehistoric times. Of course, there are rare exceptions. As the blogger from TBRDR.com puts it:[1]

> *"I'm sure somewhere out there is some guy who doesn't look at porn, and two things are true about him:*
>> *He is the extreme exception to the rule.*
>> *I'd never let him babysit."*

Perhaps my statement seems simplistic, but statistics support it (see Chapter 1). So, as I have said before, accept this fact and move on.

Lesson #2: Your Man Is with You for More than Just Sex

I believe this is one of the most important lessons that all women must learn and remember. I know you will be able to identify with it. Think about it and think about your guy. What initially brought the two of you together? What attracted you to him and vice versa? Frankly speaking, a roll in bed is always a lot of fun, but I'm willing to bet that neither you nor your significant other is so one-dimensional that your relationship begins and ends with sex. You know you are a strong, confident, and intelligent woman, and the value you bring to your relationship extends well past your sexuality. Moreover, your guy knows this too, which is why the pornography he views is little more than entertainment to him.

Give your guy some credit! Take comfort and gain confidence in the fact that the man you are with doesn't see you as a mere sexual object. Even more than that, he values your abilities. He loves you for your intelligence, your sense of humor, and your passion. In short, he loves that you're the whole package: a talented and savvy woman with innumerable intangible qualities, all of which make you attractive and sought after.

Despite what many women tend to think, particularly in moments when we are feeling insecure, down on ourselves, and pessimistic, sexual attractiveness does not trump what makes us unique in the minds of our partners. Sexual attractiveness might well be the highest priority for a man when he is searching for images of a woman to "inspire" him during masturbation, but when it comes time to find a partner to bond with in a lasting and meaningful relationship, other criteria most certainly take center stage.

And that, ladies, is why your man chose you. Don't forget it!

Lesson #3: Porn Stars Aren't Really Any "Hotter" than the Rest of Us

If any profession is surrounded by more mythology and legend than that of "porn star," I can't name it. This onscreen vixen with a seemingly

FIGURE 13.1 Me with adult-industry performers Alexis Texas, Lexi Belle, and Kirsten Price after the 2012 Pink Visual "Porn Party" in Las Vegas

insatiable appetite for sex not only fascinates men and women alike, but inspires feelings of insecurity and self-doubt so intense that we rush to our bathroom mirrors and examine our bodies, identifying all the ways we don't "measure up."

Physically speaking, porn stars aren't as "perfect" as you might think, and they too love their yoga pants and the days when they can go makeup free, just like you and me. Moreover, despite what some of the more zealous feminists out there might fear, men who watch pornography also know this to be true.

If you still don't believe me—if you still think the blonde hottie onscreen is wooing your husband into contemplating nothing but her perfect breasts and her toned butt and her apparently total lack of cellulite—remember this: It's easy (and, let's face it, kind of fun) to believe that a man can't see past the feminine ideal. That he is so blinded by the touched-up, idealized depictions, and so governed by his libido, that he fails to see any imperfections in a woman. And it's true, he doesn't. He doesn't see that many porn stars actually do have love handles or cellulite. But really, ladies, your man doesn't notice any of those things when he's being intimate with you either. In his rational mind he knows that women are not perfect, but in the moment, whether it's with you or with a video he's watching, it's perfect enough.

Let me explain how something that was supposed to improve the pornography-viewing experience failed incredibly. When Blu-Ray technology was first introduced in the adult entertainment sphere, many industry professionals were really excited about it. The idea of showing greater detail and delivering higher definition had many people envisioning the possibilities—as well as the dollars that were sure to flood in once everyone had a Blu-Ray player.

But what happened? Blu-Ray, as much as it is accepted in mainstream markets, was a fantastic bust in the adult industry. Why? Because it showed *too much* detail! With Blu-Ray, the idealized woman onscreen was actually revealed to be…wait for it, girls…a *real woman* with *real flaws*. All of a sudden those imperfections were being shown in a whole new way. Technology was trumping the makeup artists. Previously hidden flaws like shaving bumps were unpopular with the fans because they distracted from the fantasy. Nowadays, many producers in the adult industry who invested heavily in Blu-Ray technology can't give their product away.

I didn't tell you about the Blu-Ray bust to make you think, "I knew it! He only wants to see perfect women! He is completely repulsed by my flaws!" Rather, I told you this to prove a point. At its core, watching porn is about engaging in a fantasy, and as good as a porn star might look in the context of a particular movie, she looks even better in the mind's eye of the viewer. It's not that the men who watch porn don't *see* the flaws; it's that for the sake of their sexual fantasies men are very adept at *overlooking* the flaws. The imagery provided by Blu-Ray injected reality into the fantasy, which took away from the make-believe experience that pornography provides.

Lesson #4: The Real Thing Is Better than Any Video

This lesson might sound pretty obvious, but I think it's important enough to repeat. Ladies, real vagina is still tops. Men will not reject actual, live sex with their partner. Ever. Even if the sex is mediocre or just a quickie, your man would still prefer to be with you any day of the week and at any hour of the day over watching performers have sex on video. It's the truth, so next time you think your man would rather watch some porn than be with you, walk up to him, tap him on the shoulder, and say, "Let's hit the sheets, buddy." See just how fast he shuts his computer off. I'm willing to bet you won't have to ask twice.

Now, I don't have any data to back up my claim, but we do get a lot of consumer feedback from website members and visitors who are willing to offer us a glimpse into their lives. In over a decade we have never had a single instance in which a customer said that watching our porn trumped the time he spent with his partner. Nor have we ever received an irate e-mail from a woman saying that her man would no longer have sex with her because he wanted to watch Pink Visual porn.

In fact, I am so confident in this assertion that I encourage you to interrupt your guy next time he is having some face time with his computer. If he rejects you, please shoot me an e-mail, but like I said before, I would be shocked if you had to repeat yourself.

Lesson #5: Keeping Your Cool: A Level-Headed Reaction to Porn Is Best

I imagine you've tried the total-freak-out approach and it hasn't worked. That's for good reason. We have probably all had a past experience in which someone made us feel bad about ourselves. If that's happened to you, it may have injected a bit of insecurity into your life. Although the feelings probably didn't last long, or even if they did, you most likely experienced some level of self-doubt, hurt, and possibly shame.

Consider how your guy feels when it comes to pornography, especially if you, as his partner, have a problem with it. For just a moment, turn the tables and think about what you did and said when you discovered him watching pornography. Did you yell at him? Did you act disgusted? Did you shame him?

Although Pink Visual has never received an e-mail from a man stating that he finds watching pornography more enjoyable than having sex with his partner, we have received e-mails from men saying they feel ashamed of watching porn after their female partner (or a female member of the houschold) discovered the evidence. Maybe she walked in on him while the viewing was taking place, or looked through his Internet browser history, or came across a DVD still in the player. Regardless of how the discovery occurred, the man was made to feel dirty, bad, or guilty about what he was doing.

Even in my own life it's interesting to witness others' reactions to learning about my job. Predictably, most men react with enthusiasm and women are more reserved. Sometimes awkward moments ensue in which I can see that the fact I said I work for an adult entertainment company has struck a nerve with a couple and injected a tough topic into the conversation.

Public discourse on the topic of porn and its role in relationships is based on the operative assumption that viewing porn is a "bad thing to do." Marriage counselors and therapists who state that pornography consumption is increasing as a factor in divorces rarely touch on the other side of the subject. Seldom addressed is the part about being shamed for watching porn and how that might play into the tension and anger in a relationship. Is it fair to blame the death of a relationship entirely on the man when his female partner simply doesn't approve of his entertainment choices?

It must be asked: Is there an alternative to shaming your man over his viewing of porn? Is there another option?

The answer, as this book has emphasized, is yes. And it doesn't even require your watching it yourself. Think about it like this: Does your partner engage in other activities that you find boring? We've all heard the term "golf widow," and I'm willing to bet that there are more than a few girls out there who don't care about professional sports or fantasy football leagues. Can you imagine making your husband or boyfriend feel horrible because he prefers movies about aliens taking over the world, or because he loves hitting the golf course with his buddies on a Saturday afternoon? No, of course you can't, not if you are in a healthy, functional relationship. You might not understand the appeal of golf or comic-book movies, and you might not choose to participate, but you would never lay a guilt trip on the man you love about his interests. So why would you do it when it comes to porn?

Sure, golf or fantasy football might be more mainstream in your eyes, and hence more acceptable. But is it really worse for your husband to spend time watching porn than to spend an afternoon on the golf course or watching football? If so, why is it worse? Is it merely because you assume that your husband is *not* fantasizing about his favorite quarterback or superhero (save Wonder Woman, that is) whereas he probably *is* fantasizing about a porn star while watching her in action? If the reason you object to your husband watching porn is, in effect, a response borne from jealousy, is it possible that your objection to porn is less about the nature of the entertainment and more about your own insecurities?

I believe that if a woman could understand her man's involvement with porn and avoid shaming him over it, not only would the relationship improve but also, as a bonus, both partners would be happier with themselves individually.

All of this goes back to my own experience of getting upset when my fiancé wanted to watch porn. Even though I've come to terms with porn, I rarely view it for my own personal satisfaction. Still, being open about it with my husband has had a positive impact on my marriage. I even used him as a source while doing research for this book and in gathering information for use at the office. That openness has benefitted our relationship, in part by allowing us to talk about any topic because no one feels they are going to be shamed or ridiculed for their viewpoint.

The lesson is simple: just as you don't want to feel embarrassed or guilty about a personal preference, neither does your guy. Even if you don't "get" the attraction of porn, know that for your partner it's simply a part of life, a basic biological response, and it shouldn't be treated like a closeted skeleton. Allow him to do his own thing on his own time, behind closed doors or when you aren't around. Trust me, your relationship will be better for it.

That's it! Just remember those five simple things, and implement some of the other tips from this book. Make your peace with porn, and enjoy your newfound self-confidence and understanding.

Afterword

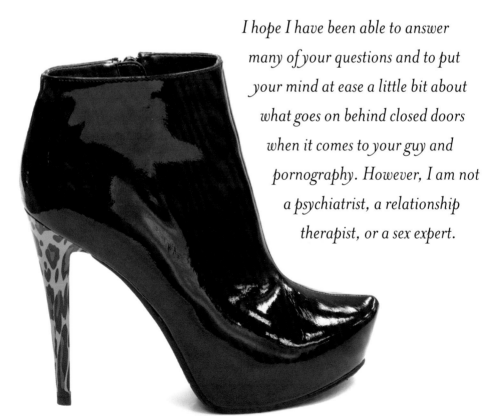

I hope I have been able to answer many of your questions and to put your mind at ease a little bit about what goes on behind closed doors when it comes to your guy and pornography. However, I am not a psychiatrist, a relationship therapist, or a sex expert.

The information presented in this book has been compiled through the resources I have as the CEO of Pink Visual, from my experience working in the adult entertainment industry, and through my own research. Perhaps you have not found the answers you were looking for or you have further concerns.

Let me say that while I personally find pornography nonthreatening and believe there are historical and biological explanations for men's enjoyment of it, I am also aware that some men have an unhealthy level of engagement with, or even an addiction to, porn. As I mentioned in Chapter 1, I have included at the end of the book a list of reliable resources that may be able to help if you still have questions or concerns about porn and its role in your relationship. The list was compiled with the same level-headed approach I used in writing this book. That is, it does *not* include organizations that will shame you or your partner, or that will inject religion, fear, or hyperbole into their attempts to help. If you are interested in finding such an organization, there are many resources available to you online.

I wish you and your partner nothing but good things. I wish you health, happiness, emotional fulfillment, and love. I hope that you have enjoyed reading this book as much I did writing it.

Best,

NOTES

★ ★ ★

Chapter 1

1. Google Trends, http://www.google.com/trends/?q=porn,+sports ,+music,+iphone&ctab=0&geo=all&date=all&sort=0 (accessed March 1, 2013).

2. Google Trends, http://www.google.com/trends/explore#q=super%20 bowl%2C%20xxx%2C%20porn&date=today%2012-m&cmpt=q (accessed March 1, 2013).

3. ExtremeTech.com, http://www.extremetech.com/computing/123929 -just-how-big-are-porn-sites (accessed October 1, 2012).

4. EurekAlert!/AAAS, "Are the Effects of Pornography Negligible?" http://www.eurekalert.org/pub_releases/2009-12/uom-ate120109 .php (accessed October 1, 2012).

5. "The Stats on Internet Porn," *Online MBA*, June 18, 2010, http://www .onlinemba.com/blog/the-stats-on-internet-porn (accessed October 1, 2012).

6. Ibid.

7. T. Capaccio, "Missile Defense Staff Warned to Stop Surfing Porn Sites," *Bloomberg News*, August 2, 2012, http://www.bloomberg.com/news /2012-08-01/missile-defense-staff-warned-to-stop-surfing-porn-sites .html (accessed October 3, 2012).

8. D. Weiss, "When Porn and Pastors Collide," *Ministry Today,* http://min istrytodaymag.com/display.php?id=17093 (accessed October 3, 2012).

9. G. M. Hald et al., "Does Viewing Explain Doing? Assessing the Association Between Sexually Explicit Materials Use and Sexual Behaviors in a Large Sample of Dutch Adolescents and Young Adults," *The Journal of Sexual Medicine* 10, No. 5 (May 2013), DOI: 10.1111.

10. J. Viegas, "Female Sex Organs the Focus of Oldest Known Cave Art," *MSNBC*, May 14, 2012, http://www.msnbc.msn.com/id/47418532/ns /technology_and_science-science/t/female-sex-organs-focus-oldest -known-cave-art (accessed October 4, 2012).

11. A. Akbar, "How E-Readers Took the Embarrassment Out of Erotic Fiction," *The Independent*, May 14, 2012, http://www.independent.co.uk /arts-entertainment/books/features/how-ereaders-took-the-embarrass ment-out-of-erotic-fiction-7743289.html (accessed October 4, 2012).

Chapter 3

1. R. Black, "Prehistoric Siltstone Phallus, the World's Oldest Sex Toy, Was Also Used as Tool to Ignite Fires," *NY Daily News*, May 17, 2010, http://articles.nydailynews.com/2010-05-17/entertainment/27064662_1_toy-phallus-tool (accessed October 25, 2012).
2. V. Socks, "Oldest Depiction of Female Form Shows that Modern Archaeologists Are Pornsick Misogynists," *Reclusive Leftist*, May 14, 2009, http://www.reclusiveleftist.com/2009/05/14/oldest-depiction-of-female-form-shows-that-modern-archaeologists-are-pornsick-misogynists (accessed October 27, 2012).
3. J. R. Clarke, *Roman Sex: 100 BC to AD 250* (New York: Harry N. Abrams, 2003), 168; C. Rodley et al. (directors), M. Milgrom et al. (cast), *Pornography: The Secret History of Civilization* (DVD), (Port Washington, NY: Koch Vision, 2006); and S. Hemingway, "Roman Erotic Art," *Sculpture Review* (2004) 53, No. 4:10–15.
4. E. Lipton, *Alias Olympia: A Woman's Search for Manet's Notorious Model and Her Own Desire* (Ithaca, NY: Cornell University Press, 1999).
5. O. Ghraieb, "New Internet Censorship Rules Take Effect in Gaza," *The Jerusalem Post*, September 3, 2012, http://www.jpost.com/MiddleEast/Article.aspx?id=283673 (accessed October 19, 2012).
6. Rodley et al., *Pornography: The Secret History of Civilization* (DVD).
7. S. Bottomore et al., eds, "Léar (Albert Kirchner)," *Who's Who of Victorian Cinema* (London: British Film Institute, 1996).
8. Wikipedia, http://en.wikipedia.org/wiki/Johann_Schwarzer (accessed October 16, 2012).
9. D. McGillivray, *Doing Rude Things: The History of the British Sex Film 1957–1981* (London: Sun Tavern Fields Books, 1992).
10. K. Whitebloom, "The Curious Case of *I Am Curious*," Boston TV News Digital Library, August 10, 2011, http://bostonlocaltv.org/2011/08/the-curious-case-of-i-am-curious (accessed December 4, 2012).
11. *Miller v. California*. U.S. Supreme Court, 1973.
12. EurekAlert!/AAAS, "Are the Effects of Pornography Negligible?" http://www.eurekalert.org/pub_releases/2009-12/uom-ate120109.php (accessed October 1, 2012).

Chapter 4

1. K. Samuelson, "Bulls and Bears: How Do Men and Women Compare in Investing?" *Chicago Tribune*, February 12, 2012, http://articles.chicagotribune.com/2012-02-12/business/ct-biz-0212-outside-opinion-male

-female-investing-20120212_1_men-and-women-daniela-schreier
-financial-adviser (accessed October 26, 2012).

2. H. E. Fisher, "The Natural Leadership Talents of Women." In *Enlightened Power: How Women Are Transforming the Practice of Leadership.* Coughlin, L., et al., eds. (San Francisco, CA: Jossey-Bass, 2007), http://www.helenfisher.com/downloads/articles/07leadership.pdf (accessed October 26, 2012).

3. A. Landers, *Chicago Sun Times* and Syndicated *Daily News Column,* January 15, 1985.

4. "Study: 40 Percent of Women Report Sexual Problems, Most Don't Care," FoxNews.com, http://www.foxnews.com/story/0,2933,445552,00.html (accessed February 5, 2013).

Chapter 5

1. Askmen.com, http://www.askmen.com/dating/love_tip_250/272_love_tip.html (accessed October 20, 2012).

2. L. A. Johnson, "Sexy Scents: The Nose Knows the Best Sensory Stimuli," *Post-Gazette.com*, February 14, 2001, http://old.post-gazette.com/magazine/20010214scentoflove2.asp (accessed October 26, 2012).

3. Ibid.

4. D. Mendoza, "Music More Sexually Arousing Than Touch, Study Says," *CNN*, http://www.wcti12.com/news/technology/Music-more-sexually-arousing-than-touch-study-says/-/13530422/17116644/-/7bkp5pz/-/index.html (accessed October 26, 2012).

5. S. Hamann et al., "Men and Women Differ in Amygdala Response to Visual Sexual Stimuli," *Nature Neuroscience* 7, No. 4 (April 2004): 411–16.

6. Ibid.

7. Ibid.

8. D. K. Hoh, "Ejaculating More Is No Cancer Risk," ABC News, http://abcnews.go.com/Health/Technology/story?id=118242&page=1#.UWNED6sjrjM (accessed October 27, 2012).

9. J. Knowles, "Masturbation: From Stigma to Sexual Health," Planned Parenthood Federation of America, Inc., White Paper, November 2002, http://www.plannedparenthood.org/files/PPFA/masturbation_11-02.pdf (accessed October 10, 2012).

10. W. Harms, "Researchers Publish New Study on Sexual Dysfunction," *The University of Chicago Chronicle* (February 18, 1999) 18, No. 10, http://chronicle.uchicago.edu/990218/dysfunction.shtml (accessed October 10, 2012).

11. Sinikka Elliot and Debra Umberson, "The Performance of Desire: Gender and Sexual Negotiation in Long-Term Marriages," May 2008, http://www.ncbi.nlm.nih.gov/pmc/articles/PMC3151655 (accessed April 10, 2013).

12. R. F. Baumeister, K. R. Catanese, and K. D. Vohs, "Is There a Gender Difference in Strength of Sex Drive? Theoretical Views, Conceptual Distinctions, and a Review of Relevant Evidence," 2001, http://carlson school.umn.edu/Assets/71520.pdf (accessed April 10, 2013).

13. Natasha Burton, "Marriage Sex: The Truth About Sex After Marriage," *The Huffington Post*, http://www.huffingtonpost.com/2012/04/13 /marriage-sex_n_1422644.html (accessed April 11, 2013).

14. S. Pappas, "Fertile Imagination: Ovulating Gals Have More Sex Fantasies," *Live Science*, March 22, 2012, http://www.livescience.com/19238 -ovulation-sexual-fantasies.html (accessed October 26, 2012).

15. D. J. Ley, "Women Who Stray," *Psychology Today*, October 25, 2010, http://www.psychologytoday.com/blog/women-who-stray/201010 /fantasy-lovers (accessed October 26, 2012).

Chapter 8
1. D. Seitz, "The 8 Most Overeducated Porn Stars," *The Smoking Jacket*, January 11, 2012, http://www.thesmokingjacket.com/entertainment /the-8-most-overeducated-porn-stars (accessed October 1, 2012).

2. I. Wong, "From Pornography to Science Teacher; She Deserves a Chance," *The Daily Titan*, October 30, 2012, http://www.dailytitan .com/2012/10/from-pornography-to-science-teacher-she-deserves-a -chance (accessed January 10, 2013).

3. "Ex-Porn Star Quits School Cafeteria Job After Uproar," *FoxNews*, December 13, 2008, http://www.foxnews.com/story/0,2933,466684,00 .html (accessed October 30, 2012).

4. "Benedict Garrett, Ex-Porn Star, Stripper, Teacher, On Fired New York Guidance Counselor: 'So Bloody What,'" *Huffington Post Live*, October 16, 2012, http://www.huffingtonpost.com/2012/10/16/benedict -garrett-ex-porn-_n_1969009.html (accessed October 30, 2012).

5. K. Battista-Frazee, "Stormy Daniels on Being a Porn-Star Mom," *Daily Beast*, August 23, 2012, http://www.thedailybeast.com/articles/2012 /08/23/stormy-daniels-on-being-a-porn-star-mom.html (accessed October 20, 2012).

Chapter 9

1. "Moms with X-Rated Jobs," *Headline News with Dr. Drew,* May 2, 2012, http://www.hlntv.com/video/2012/05/01/can-you-do-porn-and-be-good-mother (accessed October 30, 2012).
2. "Adult Performer Kimberly Kupps Agrees to Obscenity Plea Deal," *Xbiz News,* February 28, 2012, http://www.xbiz.com/news/144932 (accessed October 30, 2012).

Chapter 10

1. "Relationship Reasons for Divorce," *PsychPage.com,* http://www.psychpage.com/family/mod_couples_thx/divorce.html (accessed October 31, 2012).
2. "Why Men Look at Porn," *TBRDR.com,* http://www.tbrdr.com/why-men-look-at-porn (accessed October 25, 2012).

Chapter 11

1. Jim Dryden, "Erotic Images Elicit Strong Response from Brain," June 8, 2006, http://news.wustl.edu/news/Pages/7319.aspx (accessed October 20, 2012).

Chapter 12

1. J. Abbasi, "Vibrators Boost Sexual Satisfaction, Don't Intimidate Men," *Live Science,* November 1, 2011, http://www.livescience.com/16811-vibrators-sex-toys-sexual-satisfaction.html (accessed October 16, 2012).
2. Romance literature statistics, 2011 ROMStat Report, http://www.rwa.org/cs/the_romance_genre/romance_literature_statistics/industry_statistics (accessed October 16, 2012).

Chapter 13

1. "Why Men Look at Porn," *TBRDR.com,* http://www.tbrdr.com/why-men-look-at-porn (accessed October 30, 2012).

RESOURCES

★ ★ ★

Sexual Recovery Institute
www.sexualrecovery.com/pornography-addiction.php
(866) 690-4767

National Healthy Marriage Resource Center
3 E. Main
Oklahoma City OK 73104
(404) 848-2171, ext. 243
info@healthymarriageinfo.org
www.twoofus.org/educational-content/articles/pornography-addiction
-and-your-relationship/index.aspx

COSA
9219 Katy Fwy., Ste. 212
Houston TX 77024
(866) 899-2672 (COSA)
info@cosa-recovery.org   www.cosa-recovery.org

Sexaholics Anonymous International Central Office
PO Box 3565
Brentwood TN 37024
(866) 424-8777   (615) 370-6062   Fax: (615) 370-0882
saico@sa.org   www.sa.org/index.php

Sex Addicts Anonymous (SAA)
ISO of SAA
PO Box 70949
Houston TX 77270
(800) 477-8191
info@saa-recovery.org   http://saa-recovery.org

Sexual Compulsives Anonymous (SCA)
PO Box 1585, Old Chelsea Station
New York NY 10011
(800) 977-HEAL (4325)
International: +1-212-606-3778
Atlanta, GA: (404) 239-8048
Chicago, IL: (773) 243-2301
Kansas City, MO: (816) 374-5909

Las Cruces, NM: (575) 635-4902
Los Angeles, CA: (310) 859-5585
Los Angeles (Español): (818) 660-5034
Milwaukee, WI: (414) 963-1189
New York, NY: (212) 439-1123
Orange County, CA: (714) 664-5105
San Diego, CA: (619) 786-2722
Washington, DC: (202) 736-3736
www.sca-recovery.org/index.htm

Sexual Recovery Anonymous (SRA)
General Service Board, Inc.
PO Box 178
New York NY 10276
info@sexualrecovery.org   www.sexualrecovery.org
SRA New York Tri-State Intergroup
PO Box 73
New York NY 10024
24-Hour Recorded Information: (646) 450-9690
SRA Intergroup Los Angeles Area
24-Hour Recorded Information: (323) 850-8565
www.sexualrecovery.org

Sex and Love Addicts Anonymous
www.slaafws.org

Recovering Couples Anonymous
P.O. Box 11029
Oakland CA 94611
(877) 663-2317   (781) 794-1456
www.recovering-couples.org/index.php

The Society for the Advancement of Sexual Health
PO Box 433
Royston GA 30662
(706) 356-7031
www.sash.net

Psychology Today
http://therapists.psychologytoday.com/rms/?utm_source=PT_Psych
_Today&utm_medium=House_Link&utm_campaign=PT_TopNav
_Find_Therapist
(Offers a search tool for therapists in your area.)

Relationship Counseling Center
www.relationshipcounselingcenter.org/contact

Sex Addiction Help (California)
www.sexaddicthelp.com/index.htm

National Domestic Violence Hotline
(800) 799-SAFE (7233)
www.thehotline.org

Partners in Prevention
www.enddomesticabuse.org/index.html

Da Costa Intimacy Enhancement Trainer
www.dacostaintimacytrainer.com

Good Therapy.org
Headquarters
200 West 34th Ave., Ste. 501
Anchorage AK 99503
Regional Office
2627 Parkmont Ln. SW, Ste. 102
Olympia WA 98502
www.goodtherapy.org

Sexual Health: STD Testing, Care, and Expert Answers
www.sexualhealth.com

Council for Relationships
4025 Chestnut St.
Philadelphia PA 19104
(215) 382-6680
www.councilforrelationships.org/index.shtml

Institute for Sex Therapy (part of Council for Relationships)
207 N. Broad St., 5th Fl.
Philadelphia PA 19107
(267) 479-2391
www.councilforrelationships.org/therapy/sex-therapy.shtml

Online Couch
8200 E. Belleview Ave., Ste. 312-C
Greenwood Village CO 80111
(720) 489-5150
www.onlinecouch.com/default.html

INDEX

★ ★ ★